Charity Law and Voluntary Organisations

Report of an independent committee of inquiry set up by the National Council of Social Service, under the chairmanship of Lord Goodman, to examine the effect of charity law and practice on voluntary organisations.

Published by the
Bedford Square Press of the
National Council of Social Service,
26 Bedford Square, London WC1B 3HU

ISBN 0 7199 0910 4

Distributed by Research Publications Services Ltd,
Victoria Hall, London SE10 0RF

Printed in association with the National Westminster Bank Limited

Contents

Chairman's Preface

I was pleased to be able to accept the invitation of the NCSS to chair this Committee. It would be bogus to claim that my own exertions made more than a very modest contribution to the ultimate result but I do claim a heavy responsibility in the selection of the personnel of the committee, all of whom turned out to be absolutely first class and, notwithstanding the existence of a minority report to which I refer below, to synthesise like the ingredients in a well-cooked dish.

I did notice some criticism of the constitution of our committee based on the somewhat peculiar argument that it contained everybody except the charity-needing public. I think I can truthfully say that enough of the members have enjoyed modest personal indigence to relieve this particular shortcoming – if it was sensible to consider relieving it. The Report is a detailed one and it involved a great deal of work by the committee and especially by the two Vice-Chairmen. We have, we believe, covered in a comprehensive fashion the greater part of the subject, particularly in those areas in need of review.

It will almost certainly be the subject of criticism that we have produced no adventurous new definition of charity. Our every inclination was to do just that. We started off, or most of us did, in the firm belief that the old definitions could be discarded like old hats and in no time at all the talented milliners on the committee would produce a totally new model. Discussion and experience have taught us otherwise. There is no simple definition of a charity that would not cause many undeserving causes to qualify and a large number of deserving ones to be excluded. My personal preference was to avoid a definition but to rely on a newly constituted tribunal to determine whether an organisation qualified as a charity. I was with some difficulty dissuaded from this view point.

Although we have not achieved a new and exciting definition of charity, we have, we believe, by adopting a very detailed process of enumeration and classification, suggested a means of definition which we believe to be more appropriate and more comprehensive than exists under the present law. The principal problem in the way of a definition is the dichotomy in relation to charities between those whose objects are the relief of poverty and illness and other forms of misery and deprivation and those whose objects are of a more hedonistic nature which contribute to the quality of life. There are austere thinkers who believe that the latter category should not be charities at all but we have come down on what we hope is the side of common sense in that anything that can effectively contribute to the cause of humanity without special advantage to any individuals is in general terms eligible for consideration as a charity. It will be observed from this broad generalisation how nearly impossible it is to define a charity but it serves my present purpose.

We apologise for the length of the document. To some extent the fact that we had fallen behind our time-table has contributed to that length on the principle that 'I am sorry to have written you a long letter but I had no time to write a short one' but we do not believe that the Report is any the worse for being rather more extensively phrased than sharper editing with more time might have produced.

Finally, it is, of course, a lapse of chairmanship not to persuade or coerce the entire committee into a total unanimity of view. In the present case Mr. Whitaker has produced a minority report which is perhaps more redolent of his own individual flavouring than of any basic difference of viewpoint. We did not seek to discourage him since this particular flavouring reflects one philosophical approach that was perhaps more sparsely represented on the committee than several others, hence we welcome his individual contribution but are pleased to publish it as such.

I must conclude by expressing my profound gratitude to the members of the committee for their willingness to meet constantly and in total disregard of their professional and other commitments. They have given most generously of their time, all of them voluntarily, without any suggestion of any reward outside of the kingdom of heaven.

May I also express our very special gratitude to the NCSS, who have supplied all our needs, kept us up to the mark and ensured that the work had the highest degree of relevance that a vigilant eye and a considerable degree of knowledge will achieve and we are especially grateful to Mr. Foster Murphy, who carried the additional burden of the surveillance of this committee with an infinity of other duties so lightly that one would hardly have noticed that he was performing this massive extra task.

We are grateful indeed to Mrs. Flavia Wade for combining charm with good humour and an exceptional dedication to the job and to Messrs. Davies and Longley for their invaluable back-room support.

We hope the Report which reflects the unanimous viewpoint – pace Whitaker – of a very considerable number of highly expert lady and gentlemen will be a genuine service and that its recommendations may receive careful consideration and possibly enactment – at least in part – in the not too remote future. Finis coronat laborem.

Goodman

NCSS Committee of Inquiry into the Effect of Charity Law and Practice on Voluntary Organisations

Introduction

1. Over the past two or three years there appeared to be increasing disquiet over the effects of charity law and practice on the development of the voluntary movement. During 1973 there were repeated calls in various books, in Parliament, in the Press, and from charities and associated pressure groups themselves for the law to be reviewed. Against this background the National Council of Social Service organised a national conference in February 1974, at which almost 200 delegates from voluntary organisations and other interested parties assembled to discuss the problems of the present law. Although it was far from unanimous that any radical change in the law was needed, there was sufficient disquiet for the NCSS to take further action, the result of which was an inquiry by this independent Committee into the effect of charity law and practice on voluntary organisations.

2. The Executive Committee of the NCSS set up this Committee of Inquiry in September 1974 with the following terms of reference:

> 'In view of the present-day role of voluntary organisations within the field of social welfare,
> (a) to examine the effects of the existing legislation regarding charitable organisations in England and Wales; and
> (b) to suggest improvements which will benefit the work and development of voluntary organisations.'

The members appointed to serve were as follows:

Chairman: Lord Goodman

Vice-Chairmen: John Montgomerie, *Solicitor*
Lord Nathan, *Solicitor*

Members

W. E. Ames Lewis	Former Charity Commissioner
A. J. Balcombe, QC	
Stewart T. Bates, QC	
F. Sewell Bray	Chartered Accountant
D. G. Cracknell	General Secretary, National Children's Home
Martin H. Grundy	General Secretary, Exeter Council for Voluntary Service
Nicholas Hinton	Director, National Association for the Care and Resettlement of Offenders

David Hobman	Director, Age Concern, England
T. McMillan	Director and General Manager, Related Banking Services Division, National Westminster Bank Limited
The Hon. Mrs. Charles Morrison	Vice-Chairman, National Council of Social Service
Air Cdre. F. M. Milligan	Secretary, The Rayne Foundation
J. K. Owens	Director, National Council of Social Service
Lt.-Col. R. G. Satterthwaite	Director and General Secretary, National Playing Fields Association
Ben Whitaker	Author, 'The Foundations'
Dr. Peter O. Williams	Director, Wellcome Trust

Observer:	Adrian Longley	Legal Adviser, National Council of Social Service
Secretary:	Foster Murphy	Head, National Organisations Division, National Council of Social Service
Assistant Secretary:	Robert Davies	Assistant to the Director, National Council of Social Service
Administrative Assistant:	Flavia Wade	National Council of Social Service

3. The terms of reference refer to 'voluntary organisations', and although this term is wide and imprecise in meaning, it was purposely chosen so as not to exclude organisations which were charitable in intention, yet not in legal status, from the Committee's ambit. When the Committee was established, there was a good deal of feeling amongst voluntary organisations that the legal framework within which charities and associated voluntary organisations operate did not seem fully capable of adaptation to the changing role of charity, except by slow and costly legal and administrative procedures. A good deal of early evidence suggested that the terminology of the Elizabethan statute, and subsequent case law, were antiquated and legalistic, and inappropriate to the vital role of charities and voluntary organisations which were addressing themselves to the fundamental social problems of a society vastly different from the days in which most of the law developed. One function of the Committee was to investigate this claim and also to examine whether some voluntary organisations were excluded from charitable benefits, due to unreasonable or arbitrary rules regulating the status and activities of charities.

4. The last review of charity law and practice was conducted 25 years ago, when the government of the day set up the Committee of Inquiry under the chairmanship of the late Lord Nathan. That Committee reported in 1952 and, following the Government White Paper of 1955, the Charities Act was passed by Parliament in 1960. This Act, amongst other things, defined a charity as 'any institution . . . established for charitable purposes and . . . subject to . . . the High Court's . . . jurisdiction with respect to charities' but the meaning of 'charitable purposes' was left to rest on the existing law of England and Wales. In addition the Act strengthened the role of the Charity Commissioners and set up the Central Register of Charities.

5. Evidence was invited from any individual or organisation having an interest in the subject and having points to make by means of publicity in the Press, individual contact, and the networks of national and local organisations associated with the NCSS. Government departments, public bodies, and associations of local authorities were invited to answer specific questions. In addition, the laws relating to charity in other European countries and North America were briefly examined. The Committee are indebted to the several hundred organisations and individuals who submitted written memoranda, some of whom were invited to meetings of the Committee for oral examination. These are recorded in Appendices IV and V of this Report. The Committee are particularly indebted to the Charity Commissioners and their staff, and the staff of the Board of Inland Revenue.

6. For the earlier part of its proceedings, the Committee divided into three sub-committees, each examining that part of the law and practice in the areas of: definition of charity; financial privileges; and administration. Although the original intention was to report in under a year, members, often meeting on a weekly basis, required longer to complete the Inquiry. This was particularly unavoidable, as in the course of the Inquiry, two important events occurred. Firstly, in a number of Parliamentary Debates related to charities during the period, several points were raised on which government spokesmen made it clear that they hoped this Committee would comment. Secondly, in November 1974, the House of Commons Expenditure Committee (Education, Arts and Home Office Sub-Committee) commenced an examination of the 'Charity Commissioners and their Accountability'. The NCSS Committee of Inquiry felt obliged to consider the evidence submitted to that Sub-Committee together with the findings contained in their report published in September 1975, prior to the final drafting of their own conclusions and recommendations. (The Committee's comment on each recommendation is summarised in Appendix III.)

7. The Committee were aware that, although there are many different privileges accorded to charities, there are two main concerns which preoccupy them. Firstly, the financial privileges, which are now of the greatest significance. Although the smaller organisations may lack the

large incomes and endowments of the big charities, they are nevertheless often dependent on gaining charitable status, as such status is almost always the prerequisite for grant-aid from charitable trusts. Since these significant privileges give meaning to charitable status, the Committee focused a good deal of attention on the legislation relevant to them. Secondly, there was deep concern that charities should be guarded against undue interference from government, or attempts to distinguish between 'deserving' and 'undeserving' charities once they were conclusively proved to be charities. The Committee felt this to be an important point, as the *raison d'être* of charity is independent thought and action directed to a charitable purpose, and the Committee's deliberations are firmly based on this premise. The Committee also tackled the issue of whether the limits of charitable purposes and activities were drawn in the right place, which although a more philosophical matter, occupied a good deal of Committee discussion. It is on this point that the Committee welcomes a similar inquiry established at the same time jointly by the Carnegie UK Trust and the Joseph Rowntree Memorial Trust, under the Chairmanship of Lord Wolfenden, to examine the role and functions of voluntary organisations, in the last quarter of the twentieth century. This Committee – the Committee on Voluntary Organisations – is due to report in 1977.

8. At the beginning of the Committee's deliberations, there was an indication that there were a number of problems which might have suggested that radical reform was necessary. However, after considering the evidence and making an analysis of the problems which were discussed with a number of witnesses on several occasions, it was evident that no large problems existed, although certain areas such as political activity, procedures for rationalisation of local charities, and the administration of charities, automatically suggested themselves for close examination. The Committee were struck by the degree of confusion, as indicated in the evidence, that surrounded individuals' and organisations' perceptions of what the law and its practice meant. Some new charities, campaigning on social issues, together with several well-established charities, saw relatively few problems within the existing law; whereas others felt inhibited by the law and its practice. In the course of our deliberations we were occasionally put in the strange position of giving unofficial advice to charities on what they could or could not do. However, although we indicate a number of important changes which we consider to be essential, the Committee were of the view that no radical changes were necessary, contrary to some of the views put forward prior to the Inquiry, and indeed, the initial views of several Committee members. The Committee decided that, within their terms of reference, they would not endeavour to produce a comprehensive treatise on charity law and practice, but restrict themselves to an examination of the 'grey' areas, and put forward practical and realistic recommendations, which could be closely considered by both government and the voluntary movement, and on which relevant action could be taken.

9. The Committee were aware of the vast public support afforded to charities and associated voluntary organisations both in the form of voluntary work and financial support. It was an essential feature of our deliberations that public confidence in the administration and activities of both new and old charities should be preserved. Equally, the public and the charities themselves need to have full confidence in the law and the machinery established to administer it. For these reasons a number of recommendations are intended to strengthen this confidence.

Chapter 1

The Scope of Charity

Introduction

10. The concept of charity is of great antiquity and more or less universal; all the great religions enjoin their followers to give alms to the poor. The motives for charity may sometimes be to acquire merit or to earn a favoured position in the afterworld or in a reincarnation, but charitable impulses are by no means confined to followers of any particular religion or to believers in a life after death. Rather the mainspring of charity is a genuinely altruistic impulse, a desire to give money and voluntary service for the relief of those suffering from deprivation and to improve the quality of life for the community. This desire is not confined to any class or group of the population nor to any locality; it is strongly felt in most parts of Western Europe where organisations analogous to English charities are to be found, although for historical reasons the institutions are different.

11. This spontaneous desire to give is well exemplified by the response to the appeal following the Aberfan disaster in South Wales; and to the appeal for World Refugee Year in 1959, established under the auspices of the United Nations, to provide aid for millions of refugees, almost all of whom, as well as the cause of their distress, were unconnected with this country. Indeed experience has shown that, perhaps particularly amongst the young, there has, over the past years, been a growing disposition to give service and money for social welfare aid abroad. This probably stems in part from the feeling that in this country, the relief of poverty and the promotion of social welfare are now largely functions of the Welfare State. Even so these purposes do attract much voluntary service of all age groups in this country and the aggregate amount of money given and effort expended by those providing such services is considerable.

Development of the Concept of Charity

12. The practice of charitable activities and the legal concept of charity developed in many ways as nation states grew and created their own identities and legal systems. Both in its legal system and in the Church/State relationship, England provided the background for the development of a quite distinctive charity law and practice. In medieval times the concept of charity was mainly developed by the Church and the Ecclesiastical Courts.

Statute of 1601

13. The Statute of Charitable Uses 1601 (which has long since been repealed) was enacted to prevent certain abuses then prevalent. The statute however contained a preamble setting out a list of matters then

considered to fall within the ambit of charity. It was drawn up at a time when the functions of the state and local administrations were rudimentary in the field of social welfare, education, and even the bare amenities of life such as highways. It represented a statement of the voluntary service to the community then practised, a statement derived itself from earlier times and indeed outlined in 'Piers Plowman'. The material part of the preamble reads as follows:

> Relief of aged, impotent and poor people ... maintenance of sick and maimed soldiers and mariners, schools of learning, free schools and scholars in universities ... repair of bridges, ports, havens, causeways, churches, sea banks and highways ... education and preferment of orphans ... the relief, stock or maintenance of houses for correction ... marriages of poor maids .... supportation, aid and help of young tradesmen, handicraftsmen and persons decayed ... relief or redemption of prisoners or captives: and aid or ease of any poor inhabitants concerning payment of fifteens, setting out of soldiers and other taxes.

14. This list was not intended to be and has not been interpreted as embodying a definition or all-embracing catalogue of charitable purposes or objects, rather it has been treated as a chart or index which enables the courts to determine whether an object is charitable either by conforming with one or more of the items in the list or by analogy. The precise scope of charity has never been defined. The courts are, and always have been, the final arbiters of what is a charitable object. It has long been established that in every doubtful case the courts must decide whether the object before them falls within the letter, the spirit or intendment of the preamble and subsequent case law.

The Pemsel Case

15. Basing themselves on the preamble and case law, first Sir Samuel Romilly in 1804 and then Lord Macnaghten in 1891 in the well-known Pemsel case attempted to classify, not define, those objects which were in law charitable. This classification reads as follows:

> 'Charity in its legal sense comprises four principal divisions – trusts for the relief of poverty, trusts for the advancement of education, trusts for the advancement of religion and trusts for other purposes beneficial to the community, not falling under any of the preceding heads.'

All four of the heads of charity outlined by Lord Macnaghten have been the subject of numerous decisions in the courts. In every case a benefit to the community is necessary. In the first three cases which deal with the relief of poverty, education and advancement of religion, benefit may be assumed providing that the section of the community to be benefited is sufficient in size. In the fourth category, other purposes beneficial to the community, the court has to decide in every case whether there is a benefit to the community within the spirit and intendment of the Act of 1601. This process is not a particularly logical one but, within this framework, charitable activity and the legal concept of charity have grown over the years.

Importance of Charitable Status

16. One of the questions to which we have given a great deal of attention is whether there is a better way of defining the scope and ambit of charity but before we can come to that we have to consider whether the result of the cases is satisfactory; whether there should be amendments in detail; or whether the whole concept is wrong and charity should either be narrowed or expanded in some more fundamental way. In this context it is necessary to consider the importance of charitable status. The principal benefits are fourfold. At Common Law, charities are given two important advantages. In the first place, charitable trusts are not allowed to fail because their objects are uncertain or the beneficiaries unidentified. If a general charitable intent is established, the doctrine of *cy-pres*[1] can be applied, so as to rearrange the terms of the charitable trust to enable the charitable fund to be applied in a way which it is thought is nearest to what the settlor or donor would have intended. In the same way, if the object has become impracticable or unattainable, the doctrine of *cy-pres* can equally be applied. In the second place, charitable trusts, unlike other trusts, do not fail if they offend against the doctrine known as the 'rule against perpetuities'. In addition charities are entitled to exemption from most forms of direct taxation by statute. This is dealt with in detail in Chapter V. Charities also benefit from the assistance given to them by the Charity Commissioners under legislation dealing with charities. They may give free advice to their trustees and help with investing their funds including common investment funds.

17. On the one hand, we had evidence suggesting that the scope of charities should be restricted to what is said to be its meaning as generally understood in its ordinary sense. In short, that it should be restricted to the relief of the poor and of people suffering from deprivation of one sort or another. On the other hand, we have had evidence suggesting that the benefits accorded to charities should be extended to other voluntary bodies which have not so far been considered to come at all within the ambit of charities. Such bodies include pressure groups and, in fact, any voluntary organisation, political or otherwise. We do not agree with either of these views and we feel that at the outset we should make clear our reasons.

Should Charity be Restricted?

18. First we deal with the suggestion that the ambit of charity should be restricted. We can understand the view that to the man in the street charity means the alleviation of distress and deprivation. In the collection of money, the use in an appeal of the word 'charity' is helpful

[1] See Chapter VII, para. 188.

in that it brings moral pressure to bear on those approached. Further, the word 'charity' evokes an element of moral uplift, a desire free of self-interest to serve less fortunate members of the community. For this reason many busy people are prepared to give their services as trustees or voluntary workers and those employed are sometimes prepared to accept salaries far below what they could earn elsewhere. Therefore it is said that the word 'charity' in law and in relation to taxation should be restricted to those purposes and activities which qualify for this moral attribution.

19. Charity will never, in our view, be altogether superseded by state activity, even in the field of poverty and social welfare. There will always be gaps in the services run by the state. Further, the voluntary services may not only be quick to identify new needs and cater for them before the necessary statutory powers can be given to the state welfare services but also may give a more individual service, less trammelled by the limitations of the rule books under which the state welfare services operate.

20. But despite the unabated need for voluntary services in the field of social welfare, the alleviation of poverty and distress by state action has caused many charitably minded people to turn to other outlets for their altruism. Thus we have seen the concept of charity expanded in the latter half of the nineteenth century to embrace objects which were considered to embody a moral purpose on the basis that the fulfilment of that moral purpose was itself beneficial to the community; for instance, for the first time, the prevention of cruelty to animals was held to be a charitable object. Again, in the twentieth century, the concept of charity was extended to the preservation of the national heritage, given special impetus by the creation of the National Trust; conservation of wild life and the environment have more recently been added to the categories of charity. As Sir Harold Wilson put it in a speech to the National Council of Social Service, as Prime Minister, on December 10 1975:

> '. . . the Welfare State, I argued in the 1940's, and argue now, does not eliminate the need for private charity, it enhances it, it releases it for those purposes to which it and it alone can make the vital contribution'.

21. There are many fields where the control which tends to go with state assistance can be unwelcome and this applies especially to the arts and provision for cultural and recreational facilities. Charity is increasingly moving into these fields and this is a development which in our opinion is to be welcomed.

Should the Concept of Charity be Expanded?

22. But then comes the question where is it to stop? Parallel to the pressure to restrict the ambit of charity, there is also the desire to extend it and to afford to all 'Non-Profit Distributing Organisations'

(NPDOs) the privileges afforded to charities. There would have to be stringent provisions to avoid abuse but otherwise the objects and activities of the NPDO would be irrelevant. Thus professional bodies, political parties and pressure groups of all sorts could be accorded the privileges now confined to charities. The attractions of such a radical course seem in the main to be the following:

1. It would obviate the difficult, if not impossible, task of trying to define charity
2. It would remove the hardship which occurs when 'purpose trusts' fail because their object is held not to be charitable
3. It would enable organisations to engage freely in political activities without forfeiting the privileges which depend upon charitable status.

23. We discuss at length later in this chapter the possibility of reaching a definition of charity, or at least of clarifying the criteria which should be applied by the courts in deciding doubtful cases, but we can see no justification for saying that the difficulties should be sidetracked by giving the same status to all NPDOs as is now given to charity. This is really to abolish altogether the concept of charity as it has developed over the centuries and to alter radically the commonly accepted meaning of charities in the minds of most people. No doubt much devoted voluntary service is given to further the cause of political parties, and those who help a particular party with money or services sincerely believe that the return of their party to power will be for the benefit of the community, but this must be at best a moot question and is a far cry from any ordinary or current legal meaning of charity. Organisations whose efforts are directed to objects such as the protection of our national heritage, the preservation of wild life and the beauty of the countryside and prevention of pollution and unnecessary destruction of buildings of architectural importance may become involved in political controversy, but they are in a somewhat different category and the objects of their concern are more within the spirit and intendment of the old Act, or in more modern words, are more in keeping with the gradual development of the concept of charity than political parties or pressure groups. The Inland Revenue also advanced arguments to show that to extend to all NPDOs the fiscal advantages now given to charities would give rise to considerable opportunities for abuse. While, therefore, we believe that the ambit of charity should remain flexible and capable of growth (and as a corollary that some objects may with time cease to be charitable), we think that the existing concept should remain despite the difficulties of definition.

Purpose Trusts

24. The point made about those trusts whose purposes are held not to be charitable because they fail on grounds of legal uncertainty is one of substance. The legal argument is that these trusts fail because the beneficiaries are a fluctuating class and therefore uncertain, or

because their objects are uncertain. This can in fact be obviated by careful drafting through the medium of a company. A simple and common course is to form a company limited by guarantee with the desired non-charitable objects and this will be perfectly valid. The long-standing invalidity of non-charitable purpose trusts now serves as a trap for the unwary and has led to much litigation. A will which provides money for the fulfilment of a purpose the testator has in mind may be attacked by disappointed beneficiaries on the grounds that the gift is void. The question before the court is whether the declared purpose is charitable, or whether the testator has declared a charitable intent. If so, the gift is valid but, if not, void. This involves the trustees in much expense and if the gift is held invalid, the clearly stated intentions of the testator will have been defeated. Since the testator's object could have been achieved by adopting a different technique, there seems no purpose in maintaining the rule as it stands. Accordingly, our recommendation is that further consideration be given by government to the validation of such 'purpose trusts'.

Political Activity

25. There is also substance in the point that the present practice or law inhibits organisations with definitely charitable objects from engaging freely in political activities. This is discussed at length in a subsequent chapter in which we suggest some liberalisation of the present law and practice, but we do not recommend that all political activities should be permissible, nor do we think it desirable to go so far as to provide that all organisations of a voluntary nature indulging in any form of political activities should be given the status of charities. While we do not advocate that NPDOs should be put in the same position as charities, this is without prejudice to any action which the Government may decide to take to assist such bodies by grant-aid, relief or in other ways.

Criteria for Charitable Status

26. We have now reached the position that the scope of charity should not be restricted (except perhaps in so far as objects which once were accepted as charitable may have in the course of time ceased to have the relevant characteristics of charity); that it should continue its natural process of development, but that it should not include all voluntary activities. How then can we distinguish charitable objects from other objects? Is it possible to frame the definition which will neatly include every object which ought to be regarded as charitable and as neatly exclude everything which ought not to be so regarded, or can we at least point to the general criteria which should govern the decision whether an object is charitable or not and leave it to the Charity Commissioners and the courts to develop the concept as they have done in the past, or is there any other way?

Benefit to the Community

27. It is clear that there must be a desire to benefit the community but many things which are far removed from charity may benefit the

community. For instance, a highly successful commercial venture, generating exports and providing massive employment is of immense benefit to the community but it is not charitable. Conversely, the importance of the tax factors to charities has led some to suggest that one should first consider what purposes or activities should be subsidised and to define charity to conform to the answer so found. To argue thus turns the argument upside down. If the field open for tax benefits is undefined, it follows that any purpose which some may consider deserving of subsidy would qualify to be regarded as charitable. But the government may choose to subsidise certain types of industry and lame ducks and public utilities which cannot be run at a profit and although these might in 1601, when they were provided, if at all, by private enterprise have been regarded as charitable, they cannot now be so regarded. It would seem therefore that the concept of charity must be confined to an object to benefit the community in certain particular ways, such as relief of distress, or deprivation, and, in its more modern manifestations, the improvement of the quality of life in relation to the arts, recreation, amenities and our national heritage.

Altruism

28. Although altruism is not definable in legal terms it is nevertheless an important element in our social thinking which makes for a better quality of life. Generally speaking, it may be said that charity and the private profit of the donor are mutually exclusive and it is for this reason that at a later part in this report we have suggested that gifts to relatives or to employees of the donor even for the relief of poverty should no longer be regarded as charitable. There are, however, a number of instances where the donor benefits and is intended to benefit in a minor way from his own gift to a charity, for instance, a contribution to the parish church to support services held there does and is frequently intended to provide religious benefit to the donor among others. A gift or subscription to a learned society frequently increases, and is intended to increase, the learning of the giver and it may indeed be that the fellows of the society are the people best equipped to benefit from its existence so that only through them will knowledge in a specialised field be put to good use for the benefit of the wider community. These are two instances of what might be termed self-help gifts. Each presently qualifies as a charity and the gift is not treated for tax purposes as a payment for value received, but as a charitable donation. In this context we deal later in our report with other forms of self-help societies, namely those consisting of persons suffering from physical or social disability constituted for mutual help and support.

Definition of Charity

29. Given these two criteria of benefit to the community and altruism, the decision in particular cases is at present left to the Charity Commissioners and the court, who refer to the preamble to the Act of 1601 as summarised by Lord Macnaghten in the Pemsel case and to as many of the hundreds of decided cases as they may feel to be relevant to the case before them. There has never been a definition of charity and

many people believe that the time has come to formulate one. Others point out that to define is to confine believing the very flexibility of the law in relation to charities is, and should continue to be, its strength. They emphasise the difficulty of finding a definition in sufficiently wide terms to encompass all that is now considered charitable, or may in the future be so considered and nothing else. There has been much concern too that if any new definition were adopted, the entire body of case law established over the centuries would cease to be relevant. On the other hand, it is said that the cases have established law which is unsatisfactory in that it is out of tune with modern modes of thought and social needs and that it is inflexible. They therefore ask for how long the legal tail is to wag the charitable dog. An example of the unsatisfactory result of referring back to the Statute of 1601 is *re Patten* [1929] 2 Ch. 276, where it was held that a gift to Sussex Cricket Club towards a fund to train youngsters to be professionals was not charitable. Romer, J, said: 'It was argued that the trust is one for the "supportation, aid and help of young tradesmen, handicraftsmen and persons decayed" within the meaning of the Statute of Elizabeth. In my opinion a professional cricketer is neither a tradesman a handicraftsman nor a person decayed . . . though undoubtedly as a result of the administration of the fund boys all of the working or lower middle classes and not well off financially may embark upon life as professional cricketers'. This case is again referred to in Chapter III where the charitable aspects of sport are considered.

30. In 1952 when the Nathan Committee Report was presented to Parliament, that Committee reported (para 128), 'It is broadly true to say that we heard no suggestion that the content of the term "charity" as at present laid down in the large volume of case law based on the preamble is either too wide or too narrow'. Accordingly, the question of a definition raised in that report did not arise from a desire to change the meaning of charity. Further, in the debates in the House of Lords in 1960, which led to the passing of the Charities Act 1960, the proposals relating to definition arose in a similar context with a bias towards broadening the scope of charity.

Case Law

31. We are in no doubt that there would be advantage in eliminating the necessity in case of doubt to refer to the wording of the preamble of the Act of 1601. To do so, however, without at the same time eliminating the force of a substantial body of case law presents considerable difficulties. The virtue of maintaining much of the existing case law is that it avoids the necessity of deciding afresh all the questions raised in those cases. The adoption of definitions logically results in future cases being decided in accordance with the definition and not in accordance with preceding decisions of case law, for a definition according to the proper meaning of that word should be all-embracing. It should be such that interpretation of the words used should only rarely be required. The courts in interpreting a definition should look only to the words in the definition and not to the cases lying behind its evolution. This

indeed is the purpose of a definition. In this context we do not believe that it is possible to formulate a definition of this sort, and we are comforted by the fact that the same conclusion was reached in the debates leading to the passing of the 1960 Act. For instance, in relation to the element of public benefit, there are a large number of cases which consider the degree of public benefit required and the nature of that public benefit whether direct or indirect. We do not think that all these cases should be swept aside, nor would it be possible without a complete codification to incorporate them in a statute. What we have done in the succeeding chapters is to consider some of the fields in which the existing case law is the subject of criticism and to suggest a number of amendments of a specific nature which could be made.

Categories of Charity

32. We have also given particular consideration to the question whether a greater degree of certainty can be introduced in relation to the categories of objects which should qualify as charitable. The preamble to the Act of 1601 is written in language inappropriate to contemporary concepts and it has led, and will lead, to mental gymnastics if it is to encompass within its terms the many forms of human endeavour now or hereafter deserving to fall within the scope of charity, while excluding those which should lie outside. What we suggest therefore would be beneficial would be to produce an updated version of the preamble to the Act of 1601 and we have therefore produced a list, in general terms, of objects deemed to be charitable (see Appendix I). It is based upon the Pemsel classification extended by references in relation to the fourth head to objects which are now considered to be within the scope of charity. It is, we hope, formulated in modern and simple language. We place particular emphasis on ensuring the continued flexibility of the law in this respect and propose that the formulation should be such as not to close the categories of charity and thus crystallise and prevent the future development of the scope of charity. As it would be made clear that this new classification is an updated version of the old classification, we do not think that the existing case law would become irrelevant.

33. It does not follow that once a precedent has been established it should be slavishly followed for ever. One of the Latin tags occasionally called in aid by the courts is *cessante ratione cessat lex ipsa*, when the reasoning behind a decision has gone, the decision itself is no longer valid. In our view the categories of charity should never be closed, but there may also be categories of charity which should become extinct. In a later part of this report we recommend the setting up of a Charities Board to assist the Charity Commission. One of its functions might be to provide expert evidence in appropriate cases.

Summary

34. We may now summarise our conclusions and recommendations in this chapter as follows:

1. We reject the proposal that the scope of charity should be restricted to the relief of poverty and deprivation and to social welfare in general. While there is still an important function for charity to perform in these fields, we believe that it has a role to play in improving the quality of life in other areas also.

2. We reject the idea of abolishing the concept of charities in favour of that of NPDOs, but we do recommend that consideration should be given to the validation of appropriate non-charitable purpose trusts.

3. We do not agree with those who say that the concept of charity is outmoded and that all its activities should be functions of the state.

4. While we cannot devise a neat encapsulated definition of charity, we recommend that the categories of charities should be re-stated in simple and modern language replacing that of the Act of 1601 and extending these to include objects now considered to be within the scope of charity. This would not make existing case law irrelevant but the courts would have more freedom to reconsider it in the context of the new categorisation.

5. Legislation should be introduced to amend the law in particular cases referred to in subsequent chapters, where we think that the case law has produced wrong results or needs clarification.

6. We recommend that the Charities Board suggested later in this report should assist the Charity Commissioners in appropriate cases to provide expert evidence.

Chapter II

Benefit to the 'Community'

The Problem

35. We pointed out in Chapter I that benefit to the 'Community' is an essential element in all charities. But it does not follow from this that every individual must benefit or be capable of benefiting from a charity. Nor on the other hand is an object charitable if its purpose is merely to benefit an individual however worthy. Between these extremes the present legal position is that some section of the community must be benefited. We have already referred to the large body of case law on this topic and in this chapter we consider some aspects of this problem. The Expenditure Committee of the House of Commons had its own comments to make on the phrase 'benefit to the community' and we refer to these in Appendix III, Recommendation 1.

36. Questions can also arise on the meaning of 'benefiting' the community. In most cases under the first three heads of Pemsel the court is ready to assume a benefit. But a value judgment has always to be made. When Bernard Shaw in his will directed the creation of a trust fund to introduce a new alphabet, it was held that, even if educational, the scheme was not of proven benefit to the community. Thus as a non-charitable purpose trust the gift failed. A community of contemplative nuns, although religious, has been held not to be charitable because no evidence of benefit to the community was forthcoming. Some specific problems of this nature are dealt with in the next chapter.

The Poor Relations Cases

37. Trusts for the relief of poverty have always been held to be charitable but it has been accepted over the centuries that, contrary to the general rule, such trusts are good charitable trusts even though neither the public generally nor any substantial section of the public is eligible for benefit. Thus a limited class of beneficiaries such as poor relations or analogous limited classes will be sufficient to enable the charity to subsist for their benefit alone. Whatever the origin of this anomaly we do not believe that it is justifiable and we recommend that it be abolished for the future.

Trusts for Employees

38. We have referred (Chapter I, para. 28) to the establishment of trusts by companies for the benefit of dependants of their employees. A trust for the poor relatives of employees has been held to be a good charitable trust, whilst a trust for the education of the children of employees was held not to be so. The distinction arose from the very anomaly to which we have referred in the preceding paragraph. On the

basis of what we say about altruism in Chapter I, para. 28, we recommend that trusts created by 'employers' for the benefit of their employees and/or their dependants whether poor or otherwise should not qualify as charities for the future. If that change were introduced the Charity Commissioners would have power under s.13(1)(e)(ii) of the Charities Act to make a *cy-pres* scheme; but as the use of that power would depend on an application being made to the Commissioners, stronger powers may be needed and these are discussed in the next paragraph.

39. The question has arisen in relation to the cases mentioned in the two foregoing paragraphs as to what should happen as regards existing charities. To deprive them immediately of charitable status might cause hardship to the beneficiaries. Accordingly they should continue for a period, say 21 years, but no additions to the funds should be made and the trustees should have an opportunity during the first seven years to apply for a scheme to widen the terms of the trust. If no scheme is applied for within the first seven years then at the end of the 21 years they should be deprived of their charitable status.

Local and Denominational Trusts

40. Trusts for the benefit of residents in a particular locality such as a parish or for the purpose of a particular religious denomination have over the centuries generally qualified as charities on the ground that they benefit a sufficient section of the community. It has been suggested to us that trusts subject to such limitations should not be recognised as charitable. Discrimination, it is argued, should be eliminated. But we believe that the motive for creating such charities is to benefit those whom the benefactor has at heart. A resident or group of residents in a particular area may well wish to benefit the inhabitants of that area and create and collect for a charity accordingly. Likewise those of some particular religious persuasion may wish to benefit their co-religionists. The mainspring of their interest is the personal connection they have with those whom they seek to benefit. We regard this as a trait to be admired rather than to be condemned.

41. We are reinforced in our view that local and denominational charities should be permitted to continue and be encouraged by the large volume of support throughout the country for such charities both in money and voluntary work. Much benefit to the community would be lost if such charities were eliminated.

Trusts for Ethnic or National Groups

42. More difficult are trusts designed to benefit people of a particular racial or national group or where the beneficiaries are confined to a single sex. In other fields the law has in recent years forbidden discrimination and a Bill now before Parliament deals with this subject in relation to charities as well. If such trusts were motivated and were effective to injure those not included within the scope of benefit they would, we think, be contrary to public policy and void. But the donor

may see a particular need experienced by a given group or object, for instance Kenyan and Ugandan Asians arriving in this country, expatriate Scots or a single sex school. Should trusts of this sort be refused charitable status while a trust for Hindus or Moslems in a given area being based on local and religious considerations would be valid? Certainly by forming the trust for the benefit of immigrants generally it could be made valid even if in practice the trusts were mainly concerned with a particular ethnic group. However, what seems a mere drafting problem may involve a question of principle. We should point out that we have no evidence of abuse in the form of deliberate discrimination being practised in the guise of charity.

43. There is ample and long-standing precedent for the creation of charities for the benefit of one sex. There is, however, so far as we are aware no precedent for the creation of a charitable trust expressed to be for the benefit of persons of a particular colour and the difficulty of definition with regard to race (apart from any other reason) has precluded limiting beneficiaries in that way. Whilst we recognise that the best of motives may well prompt the well disposed to create charitable trusts for the benefit of persons of a particular colour, we consider (quite apart from any difficulties of legal definition) that there are fundamental objections which should preclude such a possibility.

Trusts for Special Needs

44. Trusts for the benefit of classes of persons with special needs have been held charitable, even though quite a small number of persons might fall within such a class. Each case requires consideration on its merits. For instance, there is no reason in principle why people suffering from a rare disease should not be beneficiaries of a charitable trust established for their benefit. Likewise in the field of education, a small group of children by reason of some special disability may require special facilities. Equally it may be desired to provide special facilities for particularly gifted children or for education in a particular field for which the demand may not be very great, such as in playing some particular musical instrument. Provided the other requirements for charitable status are present we see no reason why the fact that there may be few eligible beneficiaries (i.e. members of the public to benefit individually) should be a bar to charitable status.

Self-Help Organisations

45. There has been a development of comparatively recent origin under which a group (large or small) of people suffering from similar disability or deprivation desire, themselves, to establish a charity for the relief of that disability or deprivation and run it. Clearly a project of this kind requires exceptionally careful supervision to ensure that those who are prompting and directing the charity are not doing so merely for their own benefit which would go directly contrary to the basic concepts of charity. However, it may well be that the conduct of a charity for the benefit of persons suffering from a particular disability can best be managed by those suffering from it themselves and

therefore eligible to benefit. To exclude, for instance, the deaf and the blind from any part in management of a charity for the benefit of the deaf and blind seems to us to be taking an extreme view. We therefore conclude that, subject to special supervision by the Charity Commission in such cases, such organisations often referred to as self-help organisations should qualify as charities provided that the objects as set out in the constitution establish that benefit is not confined to the members of the organisation but is available on ordinary tests of eligibility to all those suffering from the disability in question. We understand that the Charity Commission themselves take this view but we are not aware that the point has been tested in any recent case. We do not believe that any change in the law is required.

Charges for Services

46. Charges are made by many charities operating in different fields for the services they render. Old people's homes, youth organisations, museums, sports centres, libraries, schools and hospitals are but examples. To eliminate from charitable status all charities which charge for their services would result in restricting charities to those wealthy enough to provide their services free. The absurd result would follow that a well-endowed charity would reap all the advantages of charitable status and provide services for people with means or without, free, whilst a poorly endowed one which had to charge a contribution to those able to pay would not qualify for these advantages. The poorly endowed charity would be excluded from access to charitable funds but the wealthy would not be excluded; the wealthy charity would obtain tax reliefs but the poor one would not. The poorly endowed charity would thus have to charge more because it did not have charitable status. Accordingly we are in no doubt that the receipt by a charity of charges for services rendered should not (as it does not now) adversely affect its charitable status.

Costly Services

47. A point may however be reached where the services become for one reason or another so costly that comparatively few people can directly enjoy their benefit. At this point many people feel that to grant charitable status is unrealistic. Criticisms of this sort have been levelled in relation to public schools, hospitals and clinics and certain branches of the arts. This is a topic on which there was vigorous and prolonged discussion within the Committee. On the one hand, it can be argued that the objects of the institution and its activities should be intended directly and primarily – although not necessarily exclusively – to be of benefit to the poor. On the other hand, it is said that if the objects are proper objects of charity as education, health and encouragement of the arts undoubtedly are, and if the institutions are run not for profit but on an altruistic basis, these objects should always be accepted as charitable. We do not adopt either of these positions. We recognise that in addition to those who directly benefit from the objects of the charity, there may be indirect benefit to the community in improvements of standards and this is something which has to be taken

into account. Nevertheless, it is already a principle of charity law that a sufficient section of the community must be benefited and if the facilities offered by an institution are so expensive or in some other way so exclusive that only a small fraction of the community can enjoy the facilities, this should in our view, if it is not already the law (and there is a dearth of authority[2]), be taken into account in considering the entitlement of the institution to charitable status. It is impossible to lay down any firm rule defining the point at which an instutition should cease to be charitable. This must be left to the decision of the Charity Commission or the court as the case may be who will take into account not only the number of people who directly enjoy the facilities but any other indirect benefit to the community. It must also be borne in mind that the costliness of the services and the restrictions on the numbers of people who can benefit may depend on fluctuating economic circumstances and government policies and such temporary factors should not impair charitable status.

Hospitals

48. As already mentioned in the preceding paragraphs private hospitals and clinics which as a result of their charges are open only to the comparatively rich present problems but the principles which we have enunciated in paragraph 47 apply. Evidence was submitted that certain private hospitals are extremely expensive and in practice exclude from benefit all but the very wealthy or those who have made very substantial medical insurance provision. Thus it is argued such hospitals in fact benefit a very small section of the community and a section not selected by need or merit but by economic circumstances. Over the years increasing numbers of people have through insurance schemes provided themselves with the opportunity of hospital treatment in private institutions and the income groups from which such people are drawn cover a wide spectrum. It is exceptionally difficult therefore to decide where a line should be drawn. Economic circumstances may both increase the cost of the services and thus the premiums payable for insurance and so reduce the number of people able to participate in insurance schemes. Among private hospitals and clinics there may be variations in expensiveness and exclusiveness and it must be left to the discretion of the Charity Commission or the court to decide whether the line has been overstepped.

49. In the evidence it is further stated that these hospitals have in practice 'been established and will be run with the prime object of obtaining substantial income from private practice for the doctors attached to the clinic'. This seems to us to be an entirely different point. If the doctors are in fact running the clinic as trustees or directors and fixing their own fees at an improperly high level it seems to us that they are committing a breach of trust of exactly the same character as that we have referred to under para. 45 above relating to self-help organisations. If, however, they are paid proper remuneration according to

[2] See *re Resch's Wills Trust* [1969], 1AC514 and 544A

current standards we would see no objection to this. Indeed, we consider that all employees of charities should ideally be remunerated at a proper level and not be expected to contribute to the charity they serve by accepting uneconomic remuneration.

We are, of course, aware that there is a body of opinion concerned to eliminate private medicine and private education. This is a matter falling wholly outside the province of this Committee and must be determined according to political decision, but not in our view by depriving insitutions providing these services of charitable status.

50. We summarise our conclusions and recommendations as follows:

(a) Poor Relations – These charities are not justifiable and should therefore not be charitable henceforth.

(b) Charities for Employees by Employers – should not qualify as charities.

(c) Provision should be made in the above two cases for existing charities.

(d) Charities defined by reference to Locality, Denomination, Sex, Race or Colour – We see no difficulty about charities benefiting specific groups providing that discrimination is not the motive but charities where the beneficiaries are defined by reference to race or colour should be discouraged.

(e) Trusts for Special Needs – Provided all requirements for charitable status are present the fact that the beneficiary class may be small should as at present be no bar to charitable status.

(g) Charges for Services – The fact that an organisation may have to make charges should be no barrier to charitable status provided its objects are charitable because of their benefit to the community.

(h) Deprivation of charitable status should not be used as a way of discouraging private education or private medicine.

Chapter III

'Benefit' to the Community

In this chapter we refer to a number of matters upon which we have received evidence or on which members of the Committee have themselves raised issues.

Religion as a Charitable Object

51. Long before the Statute of 1601 it was regarded as self-evident that the advancement of religion was of benefit to the community and therefore charitable. The preamble to that statute merely mentions 'the repair of churches'. At that time religion meant the religion of the established Church. Since then wisdom has dictated that religion in the context of charity should not be confined to any particular theology but should encompass 'any particular system of faith and worship which involves the recognition on the part of a man of some higher unseen power as having control of his destiny which is entitled to reverence and worship'[1]. Thus trusts for the advancement of any of the great religions of the world are treated as charitable (and we recommend no change in this) although there have been doubts as to whether only monotheistic religions are and should be included.

New Movements

52. With the spread in recent years of adherence to moral and ethical movements which may be regarded by their followers as religion or analogous to religion, difficult questions have arisen and are likely to arise as to whether their advancement should fall within the ambit of charity.

Ethical Societies

53. For many years also there has been concern, which has recently increased that ethical and moral movements which are not founded upon a belief in a deity have not been accepted as charitable. An ethical or moral system based on agnosticism or atheism clearly cannot fall within any definition of religion; yet it may set out to promote the moral improvement of mankind which is for the benefit of the community. We consider that, in principle, the advancement of such movements should be brought within the ambit of charity subject to the provisions to which we refer below

Limitations

54. We recognise that extension of charitable status to religions beyond the established great religions of the world and to such ethical

[1] See the *Shorter Oxford Dictionary*

and philosophical systems as we have indicated raises problems of some difficulty. It may be difficult to fix a boundary beyond which an alleged religion might fail to qualify on the ground that it is fanciful or freakish. Further, benefit to the community may be difficult to assess particularly in the case of some ethical and philosophical systems. We consider that those seeking charitable status for the promotion of movements of this type whether religious or not should be required to satisfy the Charity Commissioners or the court that their advancement is for the benefit of the community according to certain basic concepts which should be established. We would not regard the number of adherents as a principal test of acceptability. We have in mind particularly that a political party should not be permitted to masquerade under the cloak of an ethical or philosophical system and thus gain charitable status. We have also in mind that however liberal or tolerant a society may be it has a duty to determine what is and what is not beneficial to it; accordingly between good and evil it cannot be neutral. It must exclude from charitable status what it regards as evil just as it can and does outlaw what it regards as detrimental to its moral welfare.

Contemplative Orders

55. Many people nowadays feel that religious contemplation is of benefit not only to those exercising that discipline but also to the wider community by the example and inspiration provided. Father Patrick Barry said[2] 'Of its very nature the exercise of religion consists before all else in those internal voluntary and free acts whereby man sets the course of his life directly towards God'. The view has therefore been expressed that contemplative orders of religious communities should contrary to existing law, be treated as charitable objects. We have much sympathy with this view. The opposing view expressed by the House of Lords in *Gilmour v Coats* [1949] AC 426 is that there is no *proven* or *provable* benefit to the community if the results of the contemplation are in no way communicated to the public. Many closed communities connected with the older Christian Churches now do involve the public in their activities and may on this basis be accepted as charitable. The problem of a purely contemplative community remains and the situation is complicated by the emergence of new communities not necessarily connected with any established religion whose main or sole activity is contemplation or meditation. The Committee found this one of the most difficult of all the problems which they considered and the general view was that a value judgment has to be made in each case by the Charity Commission or the court and views may change from time to time in the context of the general development of the concept of charity. On the specific question of whether the decision in *Gilmour v Coats* should be abrogated at the present time, the Committee was unable to reach a firm decision one way or another, but it is stressed that it is confined to purely closed communities whose sole activity is prayer and contemplation.

[2] *The Times*, 24th September 1975

56. As regards non-Christian religions, whether monotheistic or not, the questions arising from immigration persuade us that it is a good charitable object to maintain the religions practised by such groups. Many immigrants bring with them a tradition of strict religious observance. The lack of facilities for this could have serious social consequences for them.

57. We conclude that in relation to religion a value judgment has to be made as to whether there is a benefit to the community as opposed to individuals. We recommend that this same principle should apply to ethical and philosophical systems in the context in which we have referred to them earlier. The Charities Board, which we later recommend, could play an important role in this regard.

Poverty Prevention

58. There is increasing concern that charity should be devoted rather to curing the cause of distress than relieving it. Accordingly the question has been raised whether the prevention of poverty or deprivation should be a proper charitable object. The present position is that where poverty clearly exists an activity which would have an immediate and direct favourable impact on that poverty, such as the digging of wells for irrigation, is a proper charitable activity within the context of the relief of poverty.

59. We have sought to find some means by which a broader concept of the prevention of poverty could be incorporated into charity law. However it raises considerable problems. The start of a new industry in order to enrich a community would not normally be regarded as a charitable object at any rate unless actual poverty already existed in that community. There might however be a near certainty that poverty would develop in an area unless something were done, e.g. on account of the running down of an obsolescent craft industry. Remedial action, such as retraining, irrigation works or reafforrestation, might in some cases be justified under the other heads of charity, such as education or improvement of the environment. If the concept of charity is to undergo a natural process of development, this is an area where we hope the Charity Commission and the courts will admit advances.

Education

60. It would be remarkable if at this time when education is so widely regarded as one of the main foundations on which civilised life depends – let alone economic life in a technological age – advancement of education were to be withdrawn from the ambit of charity.

Any decision to phase out or curtail independent education or any forms of it would be a political one and our view is most strongly that any such policy should be implemented directly by political decision and that while independent education continues to exist it should as a general proposition remain within the ambit of charity.

61. The private system at the present day makes a very considerable contribution in the field of education. In the face of this contribution by the private sector the argument that education is so adequately provided by the state that independent education, if tolerated at all, should no longer enjoy charitable status is unacceptable to us. There was considerable feeling in the Committee, however, that a point might be reached when facilities offered by an educational establishment were so expensive or in some other way so exclusive that only a tiny fraction of the community could enjoy these facilities. In such cases there is a strong argument for saying that charitable status should not be granted. It is already part of the existing law that any charity must be for the benefit of a sufficient section of the community and this we have already dealt with in an earlier chapter. We have also pointed out (see para. 47) that the charging for services cannot preclude charitable status and that the problem of drawing a line presents great difficulties. We feel that the question whether a sufficient section of the community is benefited, having regard to all the circumstances, is one which should be left to the Charity Commissioners and the court and not dealt with by legislation. The question whether certain forms of private education should be abolished is an entirely different question and a political one and should not be accomplished indirectly by the removal of charitable status.

The Arts

62. The precise boundaries of 'education' and the recognition of 'quasi-educational' objects as coming within the fourth category of *Pemsel* has given rise to some conflicting case decisions. We believe, however, that a strain has been placed upon the interpretation of education which is greater than it can properly bear. In order to bring the arts within the scope of charity they have been regarded rather as a fringe activity of education[3]. We do not consider this to be satisfactory. We regard the promotion of the arts as undoubtedly for the benefit of the community and believe that it should be made clear that this is itself a proper charitable object. Problems of determining what falls within the description of art should not be used as an excuse for avoiding the issue. It is a matter of judgement which will no doubt vary from generation to generation. When aesthetic and artistic concepts have been under consideration by the courts they have been reluctant to make value judgments on merit and have relied on the opinion of experts to guide them. In the end, however, it is the courts and not the experts who have finally to decide. In the educational context in which these matters have arisen in the past, this problem does not seem to have given rise to great difficulty and we do not envisage that if the arts were a charitable object separate from education any greater difficulty would be encountered. Promotion of the arts is undoubtedly in our view a proper head of charity because whilst it does and is likely to continue to involve the expenditure of substantial funds by the state,

[3] For instance, *Royal Choral Society v IRC* [1943] 2 All ER 101

nevertheless we believe that private support is of great importance to preserve the independence of the arts from state control.

Research

63. Research has been recognised as a charitable object provided that it can be shown that the research is of educational value to the researcher and its fruits are disseminated to the public generally. In any restatement of the categories of charity it could well be given mention in its own right. There does not seem to be any difficulty in distinguishing in principle between charitable and commercial research activities.

Learned Societies

64. Societies constituted for the advancement of learning are also treated as charities under the umbrella of education. These societies usually consist of members or fellows having a deep knowledge in some particular field who have come together with a view to extending their knowledge. They again might be separately mentioned in any restatement. We have already dealt generally with the problems relating to self-help organisations in Chapter II.

65. There are, however, borderline cases relating to professional associations. These associations are frequently designed to achieve two distinct purposes. Firstly, they are designed to promote a knowledge of the special subjects in which that profession is concerned and is expert, and to maintain standards within the profession. Secondly, they frequently carry out the function of promoting the interests, financial and otherwise, of the members of that profession. Where the association's activities are confined to the first purpose they clearly fall within the principles applicable as described in the case of a learned society. Where they fall exclusively within the second purpose it is equally clear that they do not.

66. There are many instances where one institution carries out both purposes. It is in such cases that difficulty arises. We consider that where the predominant purpose and activity are charitable in the context indicated above an ancillary purpose involving a small proportion of the activities of the institution in non-charitable activities should not in such cases deprive the institution of charitable status. Where, however, the position is reversed so that the charitable activities are themselves ancillary to the non-charitable purposes, charitable status should not be accorded to the institution. We accept that this view (which broadly accords with current practice and law) is not entirely logical and that the boundary lines are not well defined. We believe, however, that the segregation of minor non-charitable activities would result in an unwarrantable administrative inconvenience.

67. In our view it is a question of policing to ensure that these principles are complied with and from the experience which has

accumulated over the years we doubt that this presents great problems. We recognise that this principle is easier to state than to apply but we think that the principles applicable are clear.

Propaganda

68. Sometimes what is dressed up as 'education' may be an attempt to further some commercial end. Where this is the case it is clear that charitable status should not be accorded. From this, however, there appears to have grown an attitude evinced by the Charity Commissioners and the courts that research and dissemination of its results may not be a charitable activity if it is directed to furthering a particular point of view or if it tends to establish a climate of opinion or to inculcate an attitude of mind. Such a proposition appears to us too wide. Particularly in the case of academic research knowledge is often extended as a result of contending points of view being advanced with considerable vigour until ultimately some sort of consensus emerges. For example the publication of Darwin's *Origin of Species* undoubtedly gave rise to considerable controversy and had a profound effect on human thought and action, yet there can be no doubt that the research which went into that work and its dissemination was an activity which could properly come within the ambit of charity.

It has also long been accepted that the propagation of particular religious views can be a valid charitable object and we agree with this attitude which is discussed in paragraph 51.

The cases do not give very clear guidance on this issue although in re *Arthur McDougall Fund Trusts, Thompson v Fitzgerald* [1957] 1 WLR 81 it was held that research into the art and administration of government is permissible except in so far as it is deliberately intended to further the political matters of a particular body even if all the trustees under the terms of the trust deed may have to be of a particular persuasion. The general principle seems now to be established in *The Incorporated Council of Law Reporting for England and Wales v A G* [1972] Ch 73, where it was held that the category of charitable purposes extends to the improvement of a useful branch of human knowledge and its public dissemination. It is in matters relating to political activity that the distinction between genuine objective research and propaganda has most clearly to be drawn. Organisations which stand on the borderline in this area include those formed to promote world peace or to press for the observance of a code of human rights including freedom from censorship, the release of prisoners of conscience and justice for those accused of offences against the state. Genuine and objective research into the facts relating to human behaviour at the present day and the dissemination in an impartial way of the information collated seems to us to come within the description of 'the improvement of a useful branch of human knowledge and its public dissemination' but because the publication of the facts may stir people to political activity this may be a case where it is justified to split the activities of an organisation concerned with these purposes into two parts, the charitable part concerned with objective research, dissemination of facts and perhaps also relief of distress for the families of the victims, and the non-charitable part concerned with political action to put things right. This is particularly the case where a value judgment has to be made by the Charity Commissioners or the courts as the case may be.

Sport

69. The extent to which sport is regarded as a fitting object of charity is not well settled. A gift for the encouragement of 'mere sport' was held in *re Nottage* [1895] 2 Ch 649 not to be charitable. On the other hand, a gift for the provision of a recreation ground for the inhabitants of a locality was held to be charitable in a number of cases e.g., *re Morgan* [1955] 1 WLR 738, and a gift for providing squash courts in a boarding school was equally held to be charitable on the ground that sport was part of the curriculum of such an establishment: *re Mariette* [1915] 2 Ch 284; but a training scheme for young cricketers not connected with an educational establishment was held not to be charitable in *re Patten* [1929] 2 Ch 276; and in *IRC v Baddeley* [1955] AC 572 the House of Lords appeared to reverse the decision that provision for facilities in a given area was charitable.

As a result of the doubts raised by this case, the Recreational Charities Act 1958 was passed with the intention of clarifying the situation. Section 1 of this Act provides:

> (1) Subject to the provisions of this Act, it shall be and deemed always to have been charitable to provide, or assist in the provision of facilities for recreation or other leisure-time occupation, if the facilities are provided in the interests of social welfare:
> Provided that nothing in this section shall be taken to derogate from the principle that a trust or institution to be charitable must be for the public benefit.
>
> (2) The requirement of the foregoing subsection that the facilities are provided in the interests of social welfare shall not be treated as satisfied unless –
>
> (a) the facilities are provided with the object of improving the conditions of life for the persons for whom the facilities are primarily intended; and
> (b) either
> (i) those persons have need of such facilities as aforesaid by reason of their youth, age, infirmity or disablement, poverty or social and economic circumstances; or
> (ii) the facilities are to be available to the members or female members of the public at large
>
> (3) Subject to the said requirement, subsection (1) of this section applies in particular to the provision of facilities at village halls, community centres and women's institutes, and to the provision and maintenance of grounds and buildings to be used for purposes of recreation or leisure-time occupation, and extends to the

provision of facilities for those purposes by the organising of any activity.

70. We received evidence that sport should itself be a charitable object and dissatisfaction has been expressed with the 1958 Act on the grounds that its language is vague and that it is restrictive and likely to lead to anomalies. Firstly it was suggested that, while a trust for a sports complex serving all sections of the community and providing facilities for a wide variety of sports and recreation would qualify for charitable status, sports clubs which provide similar multi-purpose facilities will not be granted that status on the ground that they restrict benefit to the members of the club. It is not at all clear how far this distinction is valid. If, for instance, the East Cheam Tennis Club is open to anyone who applies to join it and if to provide for periodic replacement of its hard courts it builds up a reserve fund of investments, there seems no reason why its charitable status should not be recognised provided it has the necessary charitable attributes of altruism and benefit to a sufficient section of the community. If the club by reason of its rules is exclusive and operates a system of election to membership, it would, it seems to us, disqualify itself from claiming to be a charity.

The fact that members pay a reasonable subscription should not disqualify a club from charitable status. We have already dealt with the subject of fee paying in paragraphs 46-48. The only restrictiveness to be found in Section 1 appears to be that under subsection (2)(b)(ii) membership must be open either to both sexes or to females only and an all-male rugby club might therefore be disqualified.

The other suggestion made to us was that under the Act a trust for the facilities of one sport only would not be accepted as a charity. We cannot see any justification for this argument in the Act but if there is any doubt it should certainly be resolved possibly by further legislation. Subsection (3) envisages indoor recreations in village halls and therefore it seems clear that facilities for indoor games such as chess should be included.

71. The question remains whether other trusts for the encouragement of sport and recreation which might not take the form of providing facilities but rather grants for training or prizes should be recognised if indeed there is any doubt. We certainly think that schemes for training young people in sports should qualify for charitable status even if they are not connected with an educational establishment and we reject the proposition in *re Nottage* that the encouragement of sport is not itself a charitable object always provided, of course, that a sufficient section of the community is benefited. In view of the doubts which are unresolved by the 1958 Act, we think that the whole position relating to sport and recreation in relation to clubs should be clarified by further legislation.

Animal Charities

72. Support for charities for the prevention of cruelty to animals is

spread throughout all sections of the community and we have received no evidence in favour of excluding them from charitable status. There have, however, been certain suggestions, as we have noted elsewhere in this report, that charity should be confined to the relief of poverty and distress and it would, of course, follow that if that policy were to be pursued charities for the benefit of animals would cease to qualify. Such charities first came into existence in the nineteenth century largely based on the philosophy that they contributed to the moral improvement of mankind.

These charities have not only carried out their purpose by direct action but have been largely responsible for the initiation of legislation for the protection and prevention of cruelty to animals. The state still relies heavily upon them to assist in enforcing that legislation and some of them are active in initiating prosecutions. A change under which such charities ceased to qualify for charitable status would represent a radical departure which would not in our view accord with a wide spectrum of current opinion and we recommend that no change should be made in this respect.

73. A very different question was considered by the courts in *National Anti-Vivisection Society v IRC* [1947] AC 31. Essentially the problem in that case was that those concerned with the prevention of cruelty to animals formed a society for the purpose of promoting legislation to make the practice of vivisection illegal. There were and are, of course, strong arguments and deeply held views in support of that contention. There were and are, however, equally strong arguments and deeply held views for the continuance of vivisection. The abolition of vivisection could, of course, only be effected by legislation which would involve political activity. The court ruled that the Anti-Vivisection Society was not a charity, principally on the ground that it was directed to a political and not to a charitable purpose. Our views with regard to political activity are set out in Chapter IV of our Report. We recognise that if within the limits we have prescribed in that chapter a charity embarked upon political activity this could lead (and in the case of anti-vivisection certainly would lead) to a contest in the political sphere between two charities. For instance, a charity whose purpose was the prevention of cruelty to animals might wish to promote as an ancillary activity the abolition of vivisection whilst a charity concerned with medical research might wish to resist the passing of that legislation. We do not believe that a conflict of major principle of this kind between two charities in the political sphere should be prevented by excluding from charitable status those charities which wish to undertake such a task, provided it is clearly ancillary to and not the main object of the charities in question. We have thought it right to make our position clear in this respect because it is inherent in the proposition which we put forward in Chapter IV.

Advice Giving

74. The question whether a trust created with the object of giving

advice to the public is a charity has not been definitively answered one way or the other. While certain advice bureaux are charities, the wording used in their constitution has to be drafted with some care to achieve this result. A circuitous means of attaining charitable status of this kind seems to us intrinsically undesirable and we have therefore directed ourselves to the question whether the giving of advice generally to the public by voluntary bodies should be regarded as a charitable object or not. It has been pointed out to us that if this were not the case there would be an absurd distinction between information which can be obtained from, for instance, a public library (which is clearly a charity) and similar information given by an advice bureau which would not be. We do not consider that the comparison is entirely apt because a library will normally contain a great deal of material which may be of educational value but which could not be regarded as containing unbiased advice. It is indeed the necessity to ensure that any advice which is given to the public generally should be of an unbiased character that has concerned us most. With our increasingly complicated society involving innumerable agencies carrying out government and public purposes and with the increasing complication of law, it is more than ever necessary that the citizen should be able to ascertain what his rights are, what forms to fill in and where to send them, what organisations can give him help and numerous other matters. There is no doubt that the Citizens Advice Bureaux have provided such a service well and that this service is of very great importance in the public interest. As we have said, we are however concerned that the advice given should be unbiased. In particular, we have in mind that it should not be directed expressly or covertly to some interest which those giving the advice wish to promote such as the promotion of a particular political party or political idea. We have concluded therefore that it is desirable that the giving of advice should in appropriate cases become a charitable object and that trusts established for that purpose should be eligible for charitable status. In the light of the dangers which we have indicated, we believe that particularly careful arrangements for monitoring the operations of all charities giving advice should be considered.

Housing

75. The provision of housing for the poor, the aged and the sick is and always has been charitable, just as other relief for the poor, the aged and the sick. The development of housing associations with charitable status in order to provide housing for these classes of people has increased in recent years. This is merely a technique for providing such housing. We have no doubt that this position should be maintained.

76. It has, however, been suggested to the Committee that the provision of housing by voluntary bodies without restriction of those to benefit from it should come within the scope of charity. This proposition is supported by the contention that there is and for the foreseeable future is likely to be a continuing shortage of housing, that this is a basic requirement of society and that the provision of housing is

of benefit to the community. Special concern has been expressed regarding the difficulties encountered by newly married couples, young professional people, social welfare workers and others.

77. Voluntary housing is principally provided through housing associations. Some of these are registered charities; some are registered under the Industrial and Provident Societies Acts and are exempt from registration by the Charity Commission but are accepted as charities; while others again are not charities at all. The benefits of charitable status are primarily the opportunity of receiving funds from charitable sources to supplement the statutory funds which are available. However, the ratio of charity moneys to public funds makes the former comparatively insignificant, but they are still a useful source of extras and for associations catering for a specialist need. There is also tax relief on covenanted subscriptions, relief from the higher rates of stamp duty, rate relief and one or two other minor benefits. The principal disadvantage of charitable status is that the Inland Revenue will not allow relief unless the expenditure is for a charitable purpose, which means the provision of housing for the poor, the aged and the sick. The result is that the charitable housing associations have to adopt a particular policy in relation to tenant selection, which usually means that they must choose tenants earning less than the local average wage. Problems arise when property is purchased with some existing tenants who are not poor or where tenants who were poor cease to be poor. Many associations also want to adopt a policy of mixing tenants from varying income groups. It is for these reasons that it has been suggested that all housing associations should qualify as charitable on the ground that they are providing services beneficial to the community. If charitable status were confined to housing associations registered with the Housing Corporation under the Housing Act 1974 and if they were compelled to register with the Charity Commission, the danger of abuse would be minimised while enabling housing associations to supplement their statutory funds with funds from charitable sources. Some restriction might have to be made on the selection of tenants. They should comply with a policy to be laid down by the Housing Corporation.

78. Housing associations do not in practice relieve poverty. Their rents are fixed by rent officers regardless of the income of the tenant and it is through statutory sources in the form of rent allowances that poverty is relieved. We recommend therefore that charitable status should be granted to housing associations provided that their bona fides is established notwithstanding that in the selection of tenants they may consider housing need rather than the income of the tenants. This would not affect the position of almshouses and housing organisations not registered with the Housing Corporation if in fact they are relieving poverty.

Environment

79. The idea that the environment should be considered in the context

of charity is a comparatively modern one and has attracted much attention and considerable support in recent years. Recognition that the environment is of concern not only to owners of property but to the public generally has recently been well expressed. 'Modern man demands not only a safe and healthy but a pleasant and economically viable environment. He sees this as a human right independent of the ownership or possession of property'[2]. It is widely felt that the protection of the environment for today's use is a right of the community and that it is the community's duty to protect the environment for future generations for whom it holds it in trust.

80. The protection of the environment and the conservation of the natural heritage are, of course, closely allied concepts. Impetus was given to this movement, as has been mentioned earlier in this report, by the creation of the National Trust in 1895 and the movement has since greatly gathered force particularly in the last 20 years. 'Environment' has been interpreted in a wide sense to include the land, sea and air, fauna and flora, buildings, village greens, commons, nature reserves, even scenery, and our finite resources. It applies as much to cities and towns as to the countryside.

81. Trusts for the protection of the environment have been active and they have frequently worked closely with government (including local government) to great advantage. For instance, these trusts have provided ideas and advice in relation to drafting legislation and the formulation of government policy. There are cases, however, in which such a trust finds itself at variance with government. Such a case arose when it was proposed that a site of outstanding beauty should be utilised for the location of a construction site for oil drilling platforms in Scotland. In the planning inquiry government supported that development which was opposed successfully by the National Trust for Scotland.

82. Trusts concerned for the protection of the environment frequently intervene in planning appeals or even court proceedings. They give valuable evidence on one side or the other. They may be the only bodies with the knowledge and the funds to put the case in the public interest in which they are concerned. None of these political or semi-political activities has so far endangered their status as charities and this is right in our view.

83. Whilst the emphasis of existing trusts has been on the protection of the environment, we see no reason why charitable trusts should not have as their object the improvement of the environment. The environment is not static but is constantly changing. The shape of the countryside was radically altered by the Enclosure Acts; towns, cities and suburbs are constantly changing and thus the environment and those who live there. Charities devoted to the environment should not

[2] *English Law and the New Dimension*, Mr Justice Scarman, at p 55.

therefore be confined to preservation but should also be concerned with the manner of its development. We believe they should play a positive role by the creation of ideas and by the award of prizes and by other means for promoting a good environment. This seems to us to be particularly important in both urban and rural areas not only to encourage the development of open spaces and recreation areas but also good landscaping and architecture. There has been some activity in this field part of which may be authorised by the Recreational Charities Act 1958 and it should be made clear (in so far as it is not) that any activity not so covered should come within the scope of charity.

84. The protection and the improvement of the environment is, of course, closely allied with the public works which are referred to in the preamble to the 1601 statute. In this preamble the repair of bridges, ports, havens, causeways, sea banks and highways is included by way of example as a proper charitable object. An instance of contemporary public works carried out by a charity is the opening up of derelict internal waterways which has been carried out primarily for recreational use. It may be said that such a charity may qualify under this head or under the head of recreation (pursuant to the 1958 Act) or under the environment head including conservation of the national heritage. It does seem to us that with the potential development of fish farming in the context of the current fears of world food shortage it would be entirely appropriate that public works necessary to seal off inland waters for such development should qualify as charitable. We do not believe therefore that it is necessary or convenient that the types of public works regarded centuries ago as falling within the scope of charity should cease to do so now. We believe, indeed, that these taken in conjunction with current concern in the public interest for the environment should rather be encouraged and supported.

85. As we have indicated, trusts concerned for the protection of the environment frequently find themselves involved in the area of politics. Our views on the participation of charities in political activities are set out in Chapter IV. We believe it may be helpful here to refer to a matter which is largely confined to charities concerned for the environment. Due to the nature of their interest it can happen that such charities may feel that they should promote or oppose private bills. One instance where this happened was in the case of the Upper Teesdale Defence Fund where the fund was set up to protect rare fauna and flora in Upper Teesdale threatened with flooding by a reservoir project of the local water board. Part of these funds were applied in opposing a private bill whereby the local water board sought to obtain the requisite powers. The matter came before the Charity Commissioners who considered that the fund had been set up for a charitable purpose and the use of it to oppose the bill was a proper use. We agree with this view and that it would only be in the most exceptional circumstances that promotion of or opposition to a private bill should not be properly regarded as a charitable activity. Therefore whilst in accordance with the views we express in Chapter IV we consider that political activity carried out by

a charity must be ancillary to and not be the main object of a charitable body, we see no objection to the creation of a charitable body for the purpose of promoting or opposing a private bill in pursuance of a charitable object. We have dealt at some length with the position of environmental charities because it illustrates very well our thesis that charities have an important role to play outside the relief of poverty and deprivation.

International Activity

86. We start from the proposition that charitable endeavour is not and should not be confined within national boundaries. The relief of poverty in Africa or education in Asia concerns us in this country no less than such activities in England; nor is poverty or ignorance there less an affront to civilised thought than here. Hence a charity constituted in England should if so empowered by its constitution be as free so far as charity law is concerned to operate abroad as at home. We believe that this is in large degree reflected in the current state of the law. A more restricted view was expressed by the Charity Commissioners in their report of 1963, set out in Appendix II to this Report. In 1970 the courts decided that a gift for the purpose of planting a grove of trees in Israel was charitable, a decision which supported a substantial body of legal opinion that no distinction should be drawn as between one category of charity and another as regards activity abroad. However, some measure of doubt appears still to exist. We consider that this doubt should be dispelled in the way we have indicated.

87. We appreciate that the consequence of this might be that charitable activity abroad could be undertaken contrary to the public policy of the United Kingdom or of the country where the activity is undertaken. It seems to us that the safeguards in these respects should be clearly spelt out. We believe that the doctrine of public policy presently embodied in English law provides some protection. In principle we believe that government intervention or direction in relation to charities should be avoided wherever possible.

88. In these circumstances we recommend that where the government considers that the overseas activities of an English charity are, or may be, contrary to the public interest of the UK, there should be a procedure whereby the Foreign Office can make an order requiring the charity to stop that activity. This order should be sufficiently publicised and only made after full opportunity has been given for representations to be made including the possibility of a debate in Parliament. In deciding whether to make an order the Foreign Office would take into account representations by any foreign government.

Foreign Charities

89. Entirely different questions arise relating to bodies constituted in some foreign country who wish to carry out activities or raise money in the UK.

As the law stands at present no cognisance is taken of whether such a body is properly constituted as a charity in some other country. Such a body cannot acquire charitable status here. English foundations which have power to distribute money to charities cannot give money to foreign charities and the same rule works often in reverse so that English charities may be unable to appeal to foreign foundations.

90. The reasons for this apparently insular and nationalistic position are that the criteria for charitable status in the foreign country may be different and that the foreign charity is not under the control of our law. Neither the Charity Commissioners nor the Inland Revenue can be sure that the money given to the foreign charity is properly expended for charitable purposes. Foreign charities sometimes establish in England a charity with allied purposes which will act so far as it properly can in conjunction with the headquarters abroad. The practical objection to this course is that moneys collected in England cannot be paid across to the foreign charity because the latter *ex hypothesi* is not a charity qualified to benefit under English law. This frequently gives rise to complaint and difficulty. A solution might be to provide for registration of foreign charities with the Charity Commissioners in the same way as overseas companies can register under the Companies Acts with the Registrar of Companies. They would have to satisfy the Commissioners that their objects were charitable under English law and they would have to file accounts in this country. But there should be some mutuality in this and we would hope for conventions between states to overcome this difficulty. Until this happens we do not believe that the English courts and administration should relax the comprehensive powers they have in accordance with English law over English charities. In those circumstances we recommend that the law in this respect remains as it is.

91. There has been much concern and some evidence has been presented to us relating to international bodies such as the United Nations and its subsidiary organisations which it has been felt ought to have the benefit of charitable status in England. Some of these bodies have as their purpose the promotion of education, the relief of poverty and other purposes falling within the well-accepted heads of charity under English law and it could be argued that gifts to these institutions should be regarded as gifts for charitable purposes. For the reasons we have stated in the previous paragraph, however, we believe that the method by which this problem should be dealt with is that stated there and that no special status for the purposes of English charity law should be created for these international bodies, although there is no reason why the government should not encourage donations to these organisations.

92. Quite a separate question has been raised as to whether even promotion by an English body of understanding and friendship between nations and working for peace should be treated as a charitable object under English law. We have touched on this under the

heading of 'Propaganda'. At the present time a body constituted in England and having an educational purpose with a view to creating understanding and friendship between nations is in some cases accepted as charitable. The difficulties most often arise in connection with their political activities and this topic is considered in detail in the next chapter.

93. We may now summarise our recommendations as follows:

(1) Religion – should continue to qualify for charitable status but religions considered detrimental to the community's moral welfare should be excluded.

(2) Ethical and Moral Societies – the same principles should apply and they should also be granted charitable status.

(3) Contemplative Communities – do not normally have proper charitable objects but a value judgment has to be made in each case.

(4) Prevention of Poverty – it is impracticable to extend the prevention of poverty beyond the present practice but this is a field into which charity might extend under the process of natural growth.

(5) Education – should continue to be a recognised head of charity.

(6) The Arts – the promotion of the Arts should be a proper charitable object in its own right because it is undoubtedly for the benefit of the community. It should not be regarded as a sub-branch of education.

(7) Research – should be a charitable object in its own right.

(8) Learned Societies – should continue to enjoy charitable status if they are designed to increase the common stock of knowledge.

(9) Propaganda – the alleged distinction between education and propaganda requires further consideration but it is accepted that there are forms of both political and commercial propaganda which should be excluded.

(10) Sport – the encouragement of sport and recreation should be recognised as an independent charitable object provided the necessary elements of altruism and benefit to a sufficient section of the community are present. In so far as the existing law does not make this clear it should be amended.

(11) Animal Charities – no change should be made in the charitable status of these organisations.

(12) Advice giving – this should in appropriate cases become a charitable object.

(13) Housing –

(i) for the poor, the aged and the sick should continue to enjoy charitable status;

(ii) Housing Associations which are registered with and follow a policy of tenant selection laid down by the Housing Corporation should be recognised as charities.

(14) Charities for the Environment – these trusts should continue to enjoy charitable status and their scope should be widened.

(15) International Activity –

(i) **No distinction should be drawn between charitable activity by English charities at home and abroad. Any object charitable at home should also be considered in principle charitable when carried out abroad;**

(ii) **As regards charities which might contravene foreign public policy there should be a procedure as outlined in paragraph 89.**

(16) Charities Constituted Abroad – the law governing these should remain as it presently is but consideration should be given to allowing foreign charities to register in this country under certain conditions if mutual arrangements can be made by international convention.

Chapter IV

Political Activity

Introductory

94. It became clear from the outset of our inquiry that the relationship between charitable and political activity would be one of the most important and difficult topics for us to consider. Nor is this surprising. The reason is that the desire of charities to become involved in political action is a fairly recent development arising from rapid political and social change. Guidance has been available from the Charity Commissioners both in specific instances and generally. Where their advice has been contrary to the wishes of the charity, the charity has not taken the matter to the courts for determination; nor has disallowance of tax relief by the Inland Revenue generally been contested in the courts owing to the heavy cost of doing so. The dearth of cases relating to the relationship between charity and politics has led to a vacuum which the Charity Commissioners have endeavoured to fill by interpreting such cases as there are.

The Present Position

95. It is clear that a political purpose is not, under existing law, charitable. Lord Parker stated (in *Bowman v Secular Society Ltd* [1917] AC 406 at p442) that:

> 'A trust for the attainment of political objects has always been held invalid, not because it is illegal, for everyone is at liberty to advocate or promote by any lawful means a change in the law, but because the court has no means of judging whether a proposed change in the law will or will not be for the public benefit and therefore cannot say that a gift to secure the change is a charitable gift'.

The question remains, however, whether, and if so to what extent, political activity ancillary to a charitable purpose is permissible. The Charity Commissioners in their Annual Reports of 1969 and 1973 turn to this problem (Report of the Charity Commissioners for England and Wales, HMSO 1969 paras 7-16 and 1973 paras 7-9). The Commissioners point out that it is not easy to determine where the boundary lies between, say, permissible education of the public and political 'propaganda' which, it is said, would be in breach of trust. However, they believe that if a charity with general objects, such as the relief of poverty or distress, issues literature urging the government to take a particular course or organises sympathisers to apply pressure for that purpose to their elected representatives, the boundary would have been overstepped (1969 report para. 11). It would be no answer to say that only a small part of the charity's income had been used in that way.

The Commissioners have given examples of political activities which they believe can justifiably be regarded as being proper for a charity, which fall into three categories:

(a) Where a charity is invited by the government implicitly or explicitly to comment upon legislative proposals. Such an invitation would take the form of a Green or White Paper relative to a charity's activities, or government officials seeking advice and information from a charity. Similarly, a Member of Parliament may seek information from a charity. In other cases not involving legislation, a charity would be justified to seek to persuade a Member to support its cause in Parliament.

(b) A charity may itself or with others wish to put forward proposals for a change in the law. This can be more difficult to justify, but it is probably unobjectionable for a charity to present 'a reasoned memorandum advocating changes in the law provided that in doing so the charity is acting in furtherance of its purposes'.

However, a charity can only spend its funds on the promotion of public general legislation if in doing so it is exercising a power that is merely ancillary to its charitable purposes, and there arises immediately the question as to what is merely ancillary and what amounts to a new purpose in itself.

(c) A charity may advocate certain types of legislation which have the purpose of conferring enabling powers upon the charity (for example the Sharing of Church Buildings Act 1969). Similarly, all private bills are considered 'free from taint of political activities' and the Commissioners consider that charities should not be denied the right to promote or oppose such legislation. A charity is also considered free to promote private bills which may *set out* or alter its constitution or *give it powers which can only be conferred by Parliament.*

96. The Commissioners stressed that it is not for them to judge whether the object of a propagandist or political activity is morally or socially right or wrong. They are concerned simply with the law of charity and with seeking to ensure that funds which are impressed with charitable trusts are used for the purposes of those trusts and not for other purposes which could not be recognised as charitable.

Evidence of Charity Commissioners

97. The Charity Commissioners, in their evidence to this Committee, said that there have only been a few isolated cases in which they have felt the necessity to intervene on account of a charity taking part in political activity. On one occasion a well-known national charity had placed a page advertisement in a national newspaper urging the general public to ask their Members of Parliament to support a Private Member's motion in the House of Commons which advocated a change in government policy which the charity thought to be highly desirable and in accordance with its charitable purposes. (The arguments put forward by the Charity Commissioners and the advice of counsel obtained by the charity in this case were of great assistance to this

Committee.) Although the Charity Commissioners have publicly stated their willingness to advise trustees who are uncertain as to what the boundaries of political activity are, this offer has rarely been taken up by any charity.

Forms of Political Activity

98. The nature of 'political activity' is more easily understood than defined. Without attempting a definition we conceive that 'political activity' encompasses activity either to change or to maintain the law or government policy or action and 'government' includes local government and any organ of government. We emphasise that, contrary to a generally accepted view, 'political activity' may be designed to prevent change or to create change. Accordingly, whilst most of the charities which desire to promote change, feel themselves hampered by what they regard as the restrictive provisions of the law and practice of the Charity Commissioners, the same rules under the existing law and practice, in our view, should and probably do affect those who wish to prevent change. As matters stand therefore there is an even balance in this respect between opinions which are sometimes regarded as new and radical and those which are established and conservative. In our view any change in the present rules relating to political activity should maintain that balance.

Political Activity as Ancillary to a Charitable Object

99. It has been said that the question what is 'ancillary' is a matter of degree and therefore of judgment and we agree. Political activity in relation to a charity must, as the law stands, be ancillary to the charitable object. It is true that most political activity is, in a sense, ancillary to some other object in that the desired change in the law or government policy or action is desired not for itself but for its consequences. But in the context of a charity the activity will only be ancillary to its objects if it is designed to achieve those objects and not others which those managing the charity might think desirable.

100. It has been argued that a charity cannot attempt to persuade a government to undertake the charity's object, e.g., to relieve poverty affecting inhabitants of an area, as this would not be ancillary to the charity's objects. On the other hand, it is pointed out that a charity whose object is to relieve poverty may give money to the poor directly or give it to some other organisation relieving poverty. Why then, it is said, should it not spend money to persuade a government to do more to relieve poverty?

By and large, however, we believe that the position taken by the Charity Commissioners indicated in the foregoing paragraphs correctly represents the present law. The question arises whether this should be changed.

Can Political Objects be Charitable?

101. The first question is whether objects of a political character

should be brought within or be capable of being brought within the ambit of charity; if so, of course, any question of the rules relating to political activity ancillary to charitable objects would be irrelevant. This contention in its broadest form is that referred to in paragraph 22 and which we reject for the reasons there stated. An alternative contention is that to promote changes in the law or the policies or practices of government in accordance with the views of 'all right thinking men' should be charitable. There can, of course, be many different views as to what 'all right thinking men' do in fact or should think, which gives rise to a basic difficulty in the conception. This is so no less in the field of civil liberties than other fields. It has, however, been put to us that, for instance, compliance by this and all other countries which have adhered to the Convention on Human Rights is such a purpose and that, accordingly, political action to bring about compliance with the Convention should come within the ambit of charity.

102. The difficulty of recognising as charities organisations of this sort devoted wholly or mainly to political objects (as opposed to allowing political activity ancillary to a general charitable object) is that the organisation is almost bound to be identified with a political party, movement or group, and therefore to be involved in the quest for political power. This destroys the element of altruism inherent in the concept of charity as effectively as the quest for personal pecuniary gain. The promotion of freedom of speech, justice, clemency for prisoners of conscience or freedom to worship may be worthy candidates for charitable status. And it may be inappropriate to apply the point made by Lord Parker in *Bowman v Secular Society* to such cases. For no one can seriously suggest any doubt that a proposed change would in these cases be for the public benefit. But the dilemma remains. The alternatives are for the bodies in question to carry out their activities by means other than direct political activity, e.g., by research and dissemination of information, and only to take part in political activities to an extent which can fairly be said to be ancillary to their main object; or to separate such of their activities as may be regarded as charitable from those which are not. These alternatives are considered later in this chapter. Neither will satisfy the organisation which seeks to achieve a worthy object by wholly or mainly political means. If an organisation satisfied the Charity Commissioners (assisted by the Charities Board) or the courts that it was acting in a non-partisan way, not seeking political power for itself but only seeking to influence those in power in pursuit of an object which on a reasonable value judgment was clearly for the benefit of the community – and some aspects at least of human rights would seem to us to come within this category – we can see a strong argument for allowing charitable status. The dangers of abuse are strong, however.

Differing Viewpoints

103. The large range of evidence presented to the Committee on charities and political activity fell under three broad categories:

(a) Political activity should be outside the scope of charity. The tax benefits enjoyed by charities are provided by the community and there is no justification for activities which involve exercising pressure, directly or indirectly, on central or local government being so provided; the term 'registered charity' has come to mean something special to the general public and the willingness of the public to continue to give donations to them could be undermined to the detriment of the charities themselves if they engaged in political activity; it is difficult to reconcile the concept of trusteeship with the exercise of opportunism and expediency which characterises political manoeuvre; it would be impossible to formulate a definition which could stop political parties setting up their own trusts from which the bulk of their funds would be derived.

(b) A number of charities told the Committee that they found few problems working within the guidelines laid down by the Commissioners in their report for 1969. However, they asked for generous interpretation of such guidelines. Such organisations have acted with the understanding and support of the Commissioners but feel nevertheless that there is an element of doubt and uncertainty. Many of these charities considered that political activity which is ancillary to the pursuit of a charitable object is quite justified. However, the Committee had evidence that some charities felt themselves inhibited in their dealings with government departments and some organisations shied away from applying for charitable status because of some doubt whether their activity would be considered political so that they would not be eligible to be charities. Evidence presented on behalf of the Churches said that involvement in the realms of politics must be regarded as an essential manifestation of church life at times and nothing must be done which might hinder the Churches from organising deputations and doing what they can to influence public opinion as they did, for example, in the case of the slave trade.

(c) A further viewpoint was put to the Committee that it should be permissible for charities to pursue political objects and that charitable reliefs should be extended to organisations with political objectives. It was argued that this would invigorate political life which is to the benefit of a democratic society. By changing emphasis from 'bandaging the wounds' of society to 'preventing the injuries' there would be an acceleration in progress towards a fairer society. This viewpoint was put forward by several bodies and individuals and was not without sympathy from at least one member of the Committee.

Conclusions and Recommendations

104. In considering this matter the Committee attempted to make a distinction between on the one hand advocating or promoting the continuance or change in the law or government policy or action and support on the other hand directly or indirectly to a political party or assistance to an individual or group to obtain elective office. The Committee rejected any step which would enable charities to give

financial or other support to political parties or to individuals or groups seeking elective office. With regard to other political activity ancillary to the object of a charity, the Committee considered that there was a general lack of knowledge and understanding of the present law, many charities being under the impression that all political activity was prohibited to charities notwithstanding the contents of the Charity Commissioners' Reports referred to in paras. 95 and 96 above. There is, however, no doubt that the dearth of case law and the general nature of the guidance given by the Charity Commissioners has resulted in great uncertainty which should, if practicable, be dispelled. It is clear that a rigid approach to this problem would be inappropriate. Rather than attempting some definition of permissible political activity we believe, as at present, that each case should be considered individually but in the context of newly formulated guidelines and that political activity should be subject to review, as in other cases, as recommended in Chapters VI and VII of this report. We envisage that the guidelines should prescribe:

(a) that political activity should not be an object of the charity nor a principal activity such that its charitable object is in effect displaced by the extent of its political activity

(b) that political activity should be and be seen to be ancillary to the object of the charity

(c) that political activity should not include direct or indirect financial or other support for or opposition to any political party or individual or group seeking elective office, or any organisation having a political object.

It is neither desirable nor acceptable for political parties to emerge camouflaged as charities. The Committee has noted the special financial privileges given to political parties under Section 26(3) of the Finance Act 1975, relating to gifts to political parties and also the recent proposal to grant financial assistance to parliamentary parties. On balance the Committee considered that it is more appropriate for organisations with a political purpose to pursue the argument for financial privileges in this quarter rather than by pursuing charitable privileges. To the extent that the adoption of such guidelines involves a change in the law, legislation will be required to implement this proposal. We are, however, uncertain whether such legislation would be necessary. In those circumstances it may well be argued that it is desirable to await the outcome of decisions of the courts in the future before contemplating legislation. This, however, would expose trustees to the risk that they may be found to be acting in breach of trust and thus be made personally accountable for moneys expended in accordance with these recommendations. For their protection, therefore, legislation to clarify the position appears desirable.

105. We recognise that by maintaining a distinction between charitable and political institutions there may remain for certain bodies a problem relating to duality of function in cases where the political activity is outside the guidelines. This is, in our view, one

which has to be accepted. Where a group of people promotes a body with charitable objects and another body with political objects it is said that the division is artificial. We disagree. The two institutions have different functions which should not be confused. We would indeed prefer to see greater separation rather than unification under a charitable banner.

In reaching our conclusions, we have naturally borne in mind that the word 'charity' has a moral connotation which itself attracts support and that some are concerned that the notion of a charity being permitted to become involved in political activity may detract from the special status accorded in the minds of many to charities. We recognise, also, that the liberty to undertake political activity within the limits we envisage has for many a moral connotation. Accordingly, provided those charities which choose to embark on such activity in the context we envisage make clear to the public what the context is in relation to that charity, we believe this may enhance rather than detract from the high regard in which charities are presently held. We stress in Chapter VII of this report the need for an annual statement by charities of their activities and we consider that a statement of political activity is no less important than other activities.

Summary of Recommendations

106. **We therefore recommend that greater political activity should be permitted to charities subject to the guidelines referred to in paragraph 104.**

Chapter V

Fiscal Considerations

Background

Reliefs to Charities

107. Charities have been given relief of one sort or another against taxes since the poor law legislation of Elizabethan times. When new imposts have been introduced, it has been usual to give complete or partial relief to charities. Thus, provided that the funds of the charity are applied to charitable purposes only, there is almost complete exemption from income tax and corporation tax. The only limitation is that profits from a trade are not exempt from tax unless the trade is exercised in the course of actual carrying out of a primary purpose of the charity or the work in connection with the trade is mainly carried on by beneficiaries of the charity. Charities do not pay capital gains tax on disposals by them. Under the Community Land Act 1975, charities enjoy certain advantages, and under the Development Land Tax Act 1976 they are entitled to certain exemptions and reliefs. There are important but limited reliefs from VAT and in connection with imported goods.

Reliefs to Donors

108. There are also some reliefs given to donors to charity. If an individual executes a covenant binding himself to pay a portion of his income to a charity for a period capable of exceeding six years, he can deduct tax at the basic rate (but not at the higher rates) from his payments and retain the tax provided that the sum is paid out of his taxed income. The charity collects the tax from the Revenue. Similar provisions apply to corporations. A donor to charity does not pay capital gains tax on the increase in value of such property during his period of ownership. Provided that the gift is immediate and absolute, lifetime transfers made by donors to charity are exempt without limit from capital transfer tax. Gifts made within 12 months of the death of the donor, added to gifts made by the donor's will, are exempt up to a limit of £100,000.

Rate Reliefs

109. In addition to national taxes, charities are entitled as of right to 50% relief for rates, provided the hereditaments are occupied by the charities for charitable purposes. Local authorities may if they so wish give additional relief.

At the end of this chapter, we set out in greater detail the current statutory provisions giving these reliefs (see para. 136).

Are Reliefs (a) Justified? (b) Adequate?

110. The growing number and size of taxes from which charities are

exempt obviously makes it appropriate to consider whether such reliefs are justified or, conversely, adequate in modern conditions; whether any differentiation should be made between one class of charity and another in relation to relief; and whether, providing that the categories of charity remain roughly as they are, similar fiscal reliefs should be given to other voluntary bodies.

Amounts Involved

111. The total of fiscal reliefs must amount to a substantial figure. Relief from income tax or corporation tax of all sorts is estimated to amount to some £75m. per annum including sums amounting to £20m. to £22m. recovered under covenants by charities. No estimates are available of the value of the other reliefs. It should also be mentioned that where charities are providing services which it would be in the power of the state or a local authority to provide the charity may be able to obtain a grant towards its work (see para. 223).

Value of Benefit to the Community

112. Against this must be set the fact that the funds and assets which would incur the taxes have been voluntarily dedicated to purposes which are by definition of benefit to the community. To this must be added the immense amount of unpaid effort put into charitable work by trustees and voluntary workers. If this work were costed even on the most conservative basis, it would produce an enormous sum. Then there is the fact that much of the work is work which the state might feel it necessary to undertake itself normally at much greater expense or which otherwise would never be undertaken. We are satisfied that if a balance were drawn the advantages to the community derived from charitable funds and services would far outweigh the cost of the taxes and rates forborne. We see therefore no valid ground for reducing the reliefs or for discontinuing the practice, when new imposts are introduced, of giving favourable treatment to charities. We reject any suggestion of differentiating between charities as regards reliefs. This would give governments a political control over the activities of charities which we find entirely unacceptable. We are glad to see that the House of Commons Expenditure Committee agrees with this view. There have, however, been strong suggestions that there should be changes in the laws relating to deeds of covenant, to VAT and to rate reliefs and we consider these a little later in this chapter.

Other Voluntary Bodies

113. First, however, we should deal with the question whether similar reliefs should not be given to other voluntary bodies which may also be doing a useful job of work. We have already in Chapter I (paragraphs 22-23) explained why we do not accept that NPDOs should be given the reliefs enjoyed by charities and we have little to add here. Anyone serving the community, e.g., by running a business successfully, is in a sense a benefactor; but for the reasons stated in Chapter I it is only to those undertakings which provide a benefit to the community of a 'charitable' nature which should be given special treatment. A line has

to be drawn and we believe that if it is drawn as suggested in Chapter I with the changes recommended in Chapters II to IV, that is the right place to draw it. There is nothing to prevent governments from giving grants, subsidies, loans or reliefs to any body, voluntary or commercial, to which on political grounds it believes that aid should be forthcoming. Indeed the Finance Act 1975 exempts from capital transfer tax gifts to political parties on the same lines as gifts to charities and there is a further exemption at the discretion of the Treasury in respect of certain gifts for public benefit (independent of charitable status) connected with preservation of the environment. We believe that it is better that reliefs to appropriate non-profit distributing organisations should be afforded in this way rather than that charitable relief should be extended to organisations which are not charities or that the definition of charity should be so extended as to deprive it of its true character.

Specific Questions

114. Considerable evidence was received by the Committee on the question of the merits of the Deed of Covenant system as set against the tax deductible system operated in a number of other countries. Perhaps the largest volume of written evidence received by the whole Committee related to the need for relief on value added tax to be given to charities.

The question of rate relief also attracted a considerable amount of comment. In this section of our Report, therefore, we deal with these questions and some others which were brought to our notice.

Principles Involved

Deed of Covenant

115. The principle of allowing that for the purpose of income tax and super tax annual income disposed of under the conditions of a deed of covenant would not be deemed to be the income of the donor originates in an Act of 1803 and was consolidated by the 1922 Finance Act. There was erosion of this simple principle in later Acts. Firstly, and most importantly, in 1946 the donor became liable to surtax on the subsequent covenanted payments to charity. Secondly, in 1947 corporations became liable for profits tax on covenanted donations to charity although in 1965 covenanted payments by corporations were once again allowable against profits for corporation tax purposes, though there is, in effect, an important qualification on this in the case of closed companies – which constitute the majority of companies in the United Kingdom – and to which we shall refer later.

116. Some five or six years ago when a committee was set up by the National Council of Social Service the weight of evidence in favour of recommending a continuation of the reliefs to charities under the covenant system was substantial. More recently, however, criticism of the mechanics of this system has grown and arguments have more and more been put forward to introduce the system known as the tax allowable or tax deductible system. Basically the difference between the two systems lies in whether the donor or the beneficiary actually

receives the benefit. In the case of the British system it is clearly the beneficiary, whilst in the case of the system operating in the USA and other countries it is the donor. However, it should be noted that giving could be so arranged under either system to achieve a similar result. A similar result is not achieved at the present time because, under the British system, the individual donor has to pay higher rates of tax on the amounts he pays to charity under covenant. The significance of this will be appreciated from the table set out below.

In other countries the donor gives the gross sum and the tax on it is allowed as a legitimate deduction to be set against tax in the following year. The extent of this allowance varies; the gross sum allowed as a deduction is: in Canada 10%, in Germany 5% (or 2% of turnover). A similar result in both systems would be achieved if, under the British system, individual covenantors were allowed to deduct tax for higher rate purposes so that the total of taxable income is reduced. Of course, if this was accepted, we would expect a limitation on the extent of the deduction for higher rate purposes, as is effectively done in other countries. No doubt a limit would have to be placed on the total income.

	Gross Income Devoted to Charity	Actually Paid to Charity	Tax Reclaimed by Charity	Total Benefit to Charity
	£	£	£	£
Basic Rate	100	65	35	100
Taxpayers	1,000	650	350	1,000
50% Taxpayers	130	65	35	100
	1,300	650	350	1,000
83% Taxpayers	382	65	35	100
	3,820	650	350	1,000
98% Taxpayers	3,250	65	35	100
	32,500	650	350	1,000

This table illustrates that those paying tax at the higher rates have to devote substantially more of their income to a charity than is received by the charity. For example, a person who pays tax at the rate of 83% has to earn £3,820 in order to provide a charity with £1,000.

Tax Deductible System

117. On the one hand, the system favoured in other countries seems to have the advantage that an incentive to give is based on the expectation of recovering something from the Revenue. This advantage applies to single and to regular gifts up to a fixed percentage of total income. Perhaps the strongest advantage is that the donor does not have to commit himself for a period of years. Taking into account the uncertainties of the present time which are likely to continue and the frequent changes in taxation law, this is perhaps a very weighty argument. Spontaneous giving to charity may also be encouraged.

The main disadvantage of this system on the other hand, from the point of view of charities, is that they do not have the security of a continuity of income and this necessitates effort and cost being incurred in annual fund-raising programmes. Countries operating the system only allow donations amounting to a small percentage of a company's profits.

UK System

118. By contrast, the rules in the UK governing corporate covenanted donations to charity are more generous; unlimited donations to charity are allowable against profits for corporation tax relief for companies. But as a matter of fact, corporate giving (except in cases of companies established by charities) is small. Further, in the case of close companies, the amount of any covenanted donation is treated in proportionate shares as the income of the members of the company for the purposes of tax at the higher rate. Receiving charities have a tax advantage depending on the basic rate of income tax in the case of individuals and the rate of corporation tax in the case of companies on all net gifts under covenant. The covenanted income becomes the charity's income for tax purposes and, as the charity is exempt from tax, any tax paid in respect of that income is recovered from the Revenue.

119. The importance of security of or continuity of income to charities is also instanced as an argument in favour of the covenant system, although this may now be less strong with rising inflation rates. Where a charity concentrates its fund raising efforts over seven years to gain new covenants or a renewal of old covenants there can be a saving in fund raising costs.

120. The disadvantages of the system are that the period of seven years is a very long one and that nowadays people are much less ready to enter into a seven year obligation. Over the recent past the shrinkage in disposable income of those who were previously inclined to enter into covenants is most noticeable. However it is not widely known that a covenant need not last for a period exceeding six years. It is only necessary that it is capable of lasting for such a period. Thus it is possible to draft a deed for seven years or for some other period, whichever is the shorter, relating to the donor's circumstances but outside his control. These limiting factors can also be related to companies.

121. A second argument against the system is that the burden of servicing the covenants, collecting certificates of deduction of tax and recovering the tax could be regarded as cumbersome and restrictive. Some witnesses have said that the administration of covenant income involves the charity in considerable expense. It has been further said that there are few professionals who have specialised in this aspect of taxation legislation, therefore the system is not fully understood and only partially applied

Application of Charitable Funds' Income

122. There are many trust funds which are established for exclusively

charitable purposes. Covenanted donations to such funds constitute income of the charity and, of course, enjoy tax exemptions. And the increase from the capital of such funds is also exempted from tax, so long as it is applied for charitable purposes only.

Not infrequently such trust funds make regular, although discretionary, payments to individuals in pursuit of their charitable objects. A notable example is the payments by the trustees of the trust fund established in favour of thalidomide children and accepted by the authorities as charitable. In a Press Release dated 25th October, 1974, from HM Treasury, it was pointed out that some payments from the trust would rank as the children's income for tax purposes, some would not. Regular cash payments to the children would normally be taxable. In *Stedeford v Beloe*, 1932 AC 388, the House of Lords held that an annual pension to a retired headmaster was not income for tax purposes because, essentially, it was a mere voluntary gift. The distinction between the headmaster's pension and the regular cash payments to the thalidomide children is not clear to us, given that the payments to the children, though regular, were discretionary and in pursuit of the charitable objects of the trust. Many charities in making regular though wholly discretionary payments to individuals in pursuit of their charitable objects proceed, we apprehend, on the understanding that the payments are not taxable in the hands of the recipients. If this is not the law, we recommend that it should be. Further, even in the case where there is a commitment to make annual payments to a beneficiary under a charitable trust, we do not consider that such payments should be treated as taxable income in the hands of the beneficiary. This seems to us to defeat the object of the exemption from tax of the income of the charity. The beneficiary is, after all, the charitable object.

Conclusions

123. Having considered all the evidence the Committee reached the conclusion that the best solution would be to retain the present system, subject to its recommendation that covenanted donations by individuals should be allowed as deductions in computing their total incomes for higher rate purposes, up to a possible maximum of their total incomes. They do not think that the arguments for giving relief to the donor are such that they outweigh the considerations favouring the present system. There is no evidence that the value of donations would increase if the covenant system were abandoned and there is a danger that the reverse would be the case.

However the Committee are persuaded that the present seven year period is too long and we recommend that the best solution in this area would be to reduce the seven year period to a four year period and also to look for some simplification of the system.

Powers

Donations by Corporations

124. As already mentioned, payments under deed of covenant to charities are treated as charges on income and allowed as deductions

against the profits of the payer for tax purposes. Also reasonable donations not under deed of covenant to local charities which have a connection with the business of the corporate donor are, in practice, allowed as deductions in computing profits for tax purposes. Other donations would be disallowed as an expense for tax. Recognising the growth of a notion of social responsibility of industrial and commercial corporate enterprise the Committee recommend that there should be a statutory power, unless excluded by the articles of association, for companies to give up to a certain percentage of their profit to any charity or charities of their own choice independently of any covenant. The decision about such payments should lie with the board and the majority of the shareholders of the Company. It may be that, except in the case of charity companies referred to below, an overall limit by way of a fixed sum may have to be considered. Subject to such limitations, the payments should be allowed for tax.

Close Companies

125. The attention of the Committee was drawn to the present legislative position whereby potentially philanthropic close companies are dissuaded from making or increasing charitable donations since the directors would be mindful of the tax liability falling upon the shareholders. The Committee recommend that these donations should no longer be regarded as distributions to shareholders thereby attracting taxation at higher rates.

Charity Companies

126. At present it is a growing practice for charities to form separate companies for their own business purposes and to covenant the profits of the company concerned to the parent charity at the end of each financial year. This has been operated in the case of charity Christmas cards and some other trading operations. We do not consider that in the case of such companies there should be any limitations on covenanted amounts such as are referred to in paragraph 124.

127. The Committee do not want to encourage charities to offer unfair or undue competition to normal commercial trading. However, they do believe that the present practice which is mainly operated by large charities but which could also be extended to smaller charities if they were to enter into co-operative arrangements among themselves is not at present being abused. They would recommend therefore that the practice should be continued without modifications.

Effect of VAT

128. Again, this Committee had before it evidence produced by the National Council of Social Service on the subject of VAT. Conducting an exercise in sampling Binder Hamlyn in a report to the NCSS in early 1973 discovered that –

> 'the non-deductible VAT paid by charities on their purchases will exceed the benefit of the abolition of SET and purchase tax. In the case of the 52 charities in the sample the margin will be about 3.6

to 1. Charges made by charities for the work they do in pursuance of their primary purposes, e.g., the provision of board in residential accommodation, will in some cases have to have VAT added to them, often at the expense of the charity. Membership subscriptions which secure some benefit may be liable to VAT. Fund raising activities such as fetes, first nights and the sale of donated articles will attract VAT'.

A large volume of written evidence was received by the Committee relating to the need for relief from VAT. The report to the NCSS mentioned above made various recommendations concerning the application of VAT to charities. These included:

'that charities should be relieved of non-deductible input tax, which occurs only in relation to non-business activities and exempt activities and impinges directly on charities' ability to carry out their charitable functions. The fairest way to give relief would be to include charities among the local authorities and other bodies listed in Section 15(3) of the Act.

that no charity should be subjected to output tax in the course of performing its primary charitable functions: this could be achieved by zero-rating or exempting the appropriate supplies by charities'.

However, in spite of considerable negotiations with the Chancellor of the Exchequer overall relief from the effects of VAT have not been granted to charities. The concessions outlined at the end of this chapter have been given piecemeal since the introduction of the tax. Many charities in evidence have been able to demonstrate the costly effect of VAT upon their operations. They have demonstrated that when compared with selective employment tax from which they were exempt and instead of which VAT was alleged to be a partial replacement, they have lost out considerably.

Conclusions

129. Having considered the evidence the Committee endorses the case made by the Binder Hamlyn report to the NCSS and recommends that all charities should be free to reclaim VAT in excess of £25 a year on their expenses and that, as to output tax, no activity in furtherance of a charity's primary purpose should be considered as a business for VAT.

Importance of Rate Relief to Charities

130. The Committee were able to discover that in the year 1972/73 the rate income loss by county boroughs varied from 0.1 per cent of the total amount to be collected up to 2.08 per cent. There is reason to believe that such figures would apply also to other local authorities collecting rates. For charities the 50% mandatory rate relief represents an extremely important concession equally to local small and medium sized charities and to the large national organisations. Therefore the evidence received from charities on this subject suggested that there should be no change in this system and indeed that the percentage of

mandatory relief should be extended or that the level of discretionary relief should be more uniform throughout the country.

Local Authorities Views

131. On the other hand, local authority associations and some other public bodies gave reasons in evidence why the system should be changed to one under which direct grant was given to the headquarters of national charities from Central Government and rate relief should be made discretionary upon rating authorities. The point was made that mandatory relief is a hidden subsidy from the rates and that it would be far better that financial assistance should be an overt act on the part of the Government. It was also suggested that some charities enjoy rate relief in circumstances which were never in contemplation when the principle was first endorsed. Instances were given of industrial training boards which were set up with public funding. The local authority associations also pointed out that since the grant they receive from the central Government is based on rateable values and takes no account of the fact that they receive no rates from exempt properties those local authorities with a lot of charities in their area are prejudiced.

Conclusions

132. Having considered the points put on both sides, we would recommend that there should be no alteration to the principle of discretionary reliefs and are gratified to note that the Layfield Committee[1] have made the same suggestion in their Report. Like us, they do not feel that the overall level of financial relief given in this way to charities is disproportionate to the benefit that is brought to the community. However, we would want to go beyond the Layfield recommendations. We suggest that the level of discretionary and mandatory relief should be reconsidered and that the latter should be raised to 75% leaving rating authorities to give extra relief to local charities if they think fit. We also welcome the Layfield recommendation that the cost of mandatory relief should not be borne by the rating authorities themselves, but by central government.

General Service Charge

133. A second problem connected with rating results from the Water Act 1973. This Act transferred responsibility for certain general services connected with the water services (including sewerage charges) to English and Welsh Water Authorities. Under temporary arrangements, those services other than water rate which were transferred to the Water Authorities and which are based on rateable values, are presently collected by the various rating authorities on behalf of the Water Authorities. They are shown separately on the Rate Demands under the heading General Service Charge, and include, *inter alia*, charges for sewerage disposal, river maintenance, and land drainage. These charges are not eligible for rate rebates. Prior to their

[1] Local Government Finance Report of the Committee of Inquiry (Cmnd. 6453).

transfer under the provisions of the Water Act 1973, charities received relief from payment for the services now contained in the General Service Charge. Evidence was produced to the Committee as to the burden of this on charities. Relief from payment for these services by charities is a very long standing tradition: it has existed since the days of local valuation authorities and was confirmed in the present 50% mandatory relief now enjoyed. In keeping with this long standing tradition we recommend that charities should be granted relief from the General Service Charge.

Charity Shops

134. A particular problem which received attention by the Committee concerned rate relief for charity shops. In a test case between Oxfam and Birmingham City Council the House of Lords gave judgment in April 1975 that charity shops were not eligible for mandatory rate relief because the purposes for which they were being used were not 'wholly or mainly charitable'. In their judgment the Law Lords stated that they were sympathetic to the case put by Oxfam but that clearly the 1967 Act and a previous judgment relating to fund raising activities by charities as not being a wholly charitable purpose meant that they could give no other decision. In our view legislation amending Section 40 of the 1967 Act should be enacted so that fund raising would be expressly a use, in addition to uses for charitable purposes, meriting rate relief in appropriate cases. We, therefore, welcome the fact that legislation to this effect has been passed during the course of our deliberations.

Recommendations

135. We may summarise our recommendations in this chapter as follows:

(a) that the present reliefs granted to charities should be continued subject to the amendments recommended in the following sub-paragraphs.

(b) in the case of individuals, covenanted donations to charities should be allowed as deductions in computing their total incomes for higher rate tax purposes subject to a maximum limit.

(c) that the seven year period should be reduced to four, and that further simplification should be sought in the administration of the system.

(d) that regular discretionary payments by charities to individuals should not be chargeable to tax in their hands.

(e) that companies should have power, unless expressly prohibited by their constitution, to give a percentage of their profit to any charity independently of any covenant or whether or not the charity has any direct connection with the company; that subject to a maximum limit on all donations the payments should be allowed for tax; that donations by close companies within the above limits should not be regarded as distributions to shareholders.

(f) that the present practice of forming charity companies for trading purposes should not be interfered with.

(g) that all charities should be enabled to reclaim VAT in excess of £25 a year on their expenses; that for the purposes of output tax no activity in furtherance of a charity's primary purpose should be considered as a business for VAT.
(h) that rate relief to charities should continue and the mandatory rate relief should be raised to 75% to be borne centrally; that charities should be relieved from the general service charge; for the purpose of rate relief fund raising should be regarded as being as much a primary function of a charity as fund spending.

Fiscal Provisions Relating to Charities at the present moment

136. The Committee began by reviewing the position relating to fiscal benefits of charitable status. During the time in which it was sitting changes emerged relating to certain aspects, i.e., capital transfer tax and development gains on land. The position at the time of going to press is as follows:

1. **Income Tax and Corporation Tax**

The Income and Corporation Taxes Act 1970 provides:

(a) Exemption from tax under Schedule A or Schedule D on rents of land owned by a hospital, public school, or almshouse, or vested in trustees for charitable purposes so far as the rents are applied to charitable purposes only (Sect. 360 (1) (a));
(b) Exemption from tax under Schedule B on lands occupied by a charity (Section 360 (1) (a));
(c) Exemption from tax under Schedule C, Schedule D or Schedule F on interest, annuities, dividends, distributions and annual payments forming part of the income of any body of persons or trust established for charitable purposes only, or which, according to the rules or regulations established by Act of Parliament, charter, decree, deed of trust or will, are applicable to charitable purposes only and so far as the same are applied to charitable purposes only (Section 360 (1) (c)),
(d) Exemption from tax under Schedule C on interest, annuities, dividends or shares of annuities in the names of trustees applicable solely towards the repairs of any cathedral, college, church or chapel, or any building used solely for the purposes of divine worship and so far as the income is applied to those purposes (Section 360 (1) (d));
(e) Exemption from tax under Schedule D on the profits of a trade carried on by a charity if the profits are applied solely to the purposes of the charity and either –

(1) the trade is exercised in the course of the actual carrying out of a primary purpose of the charity; or
(2) the work in connection with the trade is mainly carried on by beneficiaries of the Charity (Section 360 (1) (e));

(f) That exemption from income tax shall have the like effect for the purposes of corporation tax (Section 360 (4)).

2. **Deeds of Covenant**

Where an individual executes a deed of covenant binding himself to pay a portion of his income to a charity for a period capable of exceeding six years, that part of his income is treated as being the income of the charity. In practice, the donor deducts basic rate income tax from the payments made to the charity which in turn can claim a refund of this tax. (Section 52, Income and Corporation Taxes Act (1970).)

Subject to the special case of close companies referred to in paragraphs 115 and 125, where a company enters into a deed of covenant it may deduct the gross amount of its payments from its profits before these are assessed for corporation tax. It must, however, deduct income tax at the basic rate from the gross amount before paying the charity.

As in the case of the individual's deed of covenant, the charity can claim a refund of the income tax. The company which does not normally pay income tax has to account to the Inland Revenue for the tax deducted. Deeds of covenant in favour of charities are executed at the rate of almost 400,000 per annum and produce over 2,000,000 annual payments totalling some £60 million gross.

3. **Capital Gains Tax**

(a) Section 360 (2), Income and Corporation Taxes Act 1970, provides that a charity shall in respect of tax on capital gains be allowed exemption in accordance with Section 35, Finance Act 1965.

(b) Section 119, Finance Act 1972, provides that a donor who gives property to a charity shall not be liable to a capital gains tax on the increase in value of such property during his period of ownership.

4. **Capital Transfer Tax**

The Finance Act 1975 as amended by The Finance Act 1976 effectively replaced estate duty by a capital transfer tax. Now when a person dies capital transfer tax is charged as if immediately before his death the deceased had made a transfer of value.

There are important exemptions, as noted below, which are relevant to charities. It should be observed, however, that exemption from capital transfer tax is granted only where a gift to a charity is immediate and absolute (where the gift is outright or is given in trust exclusively for charitable purposes).

(i) Gifts up to a total value of £2,000 made in any one year are exempt from capital transfer tax.

(ii) Gifts made as part of the donor's normal expenditure out of income are exempt from capital transfer tax if the donor is left with sufficient income to maintain his usual standard of living. The existence of a deed of covenant would usually imply that the giving was part of the donor's normal expenditure.

(iii) Lifetime gifts to charities made a year or more before the death of the donor are wholly exempt from capital transfer tax.

(iv) Gifts to charities made within a year of the death of the donor or by his will are exempt up to a limit of £100,000.

(v) Gifts enjoy an unlimited exemption from capital transfer tax if they are made for certain national purposes such as the National Gallery and the British Museum.

(vi) The Treasury has power to exempt, *inter alia*, gifts of Land of (in the opinion of the Treasury) outstanding scenic or historic or scientific interest; gifts of buildings of outstanding historic or architectural or aesthetic interest; property given as a source of income for the upkeep of such lands and buildings; and pictures, books, manuscripts, works of art, etc, of national or historic or scientific interest.

An exempt gift is disregarded for the purpose of calculating the rate of capital transfer tax on chargeable transfers. If part of an estate is given to a charity by will, the rate of any capital transfer tax payable on the rest of the estate will be reduced.

Married benefactors who wish a charity to benefit only after the death of themselves and their spouses, can leave their estate or a part to their spouses for life, and on the spouse's death to the charity absolutely. No capital transfer tax will become payable on the estate (or part of it) or on either death in such circumstances. Capital distributions made by charitable trusts are not subject to capital transfer tax nor are distributions made by private trusts in favour of charity treated as capital distributions.

5. **Community Land Act, 1975**

Under this Act an authority as therein defined has power to acquire any land which, in their opinion, is suitable for development. But there are provisions to relieve charities of the full effect of these land acquisition powers. And, given certain conditions, the measure of compensation payable on acquisition is more beneficial in the case of charities.

6. **Development Land Tax Act**

The Development Land Tax Act 1976, imposes a new tax on the realisation of the development value of land. In appropriate cases this effectively replaces the development gains tax which was introduced in 1974.

Land which was owned by a Charity on White Paper day (12th September 1974) –

(a) can be developed in any way without attracting the acquisition duty of the local authority, or be sold, without in either case, liability to development land tax;

(b) if acquired will be entitled to compensation based on market value for 11 years from White Paper day, or until the Second Appointed day under the Community Land Act, whichever is the later.

Land (unless it was charity land) which a charity may acquire or be given since White Paper day –

(i) may be developed for the charity's own use without liability to development land tax at the time, but the tax liability is deferred and becomes payable if and when the land is sold.

(ii) where a development takes place which is not for the 'purposes of the charity' this will incur liability to the tax.

7. **Wealth Tax**

The present Government declared their intention in a Green Paper issued in August 1974 (Cmd.5704) to introduce a wealth tax. However, paragraph 17 of that Green Paper states 'Trusts for wholly charitable purposes will in general be exempt from tax . . . '

8. **Value Added Tax**

There is no general relief for charities from this tax but the Finance Act 1972 provides for the following specific reliefs to charities:

(i) zero rating of the supply to the Royal National Institute for the Blind of talking-book machines and their related tapes, parts and accessories for use by the blind, together with similar supplies to the National Listening Library or other similar charities for use by the severely handicapped – Schedule 4 Group 4 Item 9 (as amended by the Value Added Tax (Consolidation) Order 1974).

(ii) zero rating of the supply to a charity of wireless receiving sets solely for gratuitous loan to the blind – Schedule 4 Group 4 Item 2 (as amended by the Value Added Tax (Consolidation) Order 1974).

(iii) zero rating of the supply of medical and scientific equipment where it is purchased with funds provided by a charity or from voluntary contributions and is being donated to a designated non-profit-making hospital or research institution solely for use in medical research, diagnosis or treatment – Schedule 4 Group 16 Item 3 (as amended by the Value Added Tax (Donated Medical Equipment) Order 1974).

(iv) zero rating of the supply to and repair or maintenance for the Royal National Lifeboat Institution of any lifeboat – Schedule 4 Group 10 Item 3.

Where a charity is registered for VAT purposes by virtue of the fact that it has ordinary business activities resulting in a gross turnover exceeding £5,000 a year, there are a number of other possible benefits:

(i) zero rating of the supply of any goods donated by a charity established primarily for the relief of distress – Schedule 4 Group 16 Item 1 (as amended by the Value Added Tax (Donated Medical Equipment) Order 1974).

(ii) zero rating of any goods exported by a charity whether or not exported by way of business – Schedule 4 Group 16 Item 2 (as amended by the Value Added Tax (Donated Medical Equipment) Order 1974).

(iii) zero rating, subject to certain conditions, of the supply of medical and surgical appliances etc. This relief is not specific to charities but provided the general conditions of the relief are met charities registered for the tax may gain relief by zero-rating the supply of aids and appliances to an eligible patient – Schedule 4 Group 14 (as amended by the Value Added Tax (Consolidation) Order 1974).

(iv) exemption for the provision by a youth club of the facilities available to its members – Schedule 5 Group 6 Item 4.
(v) exemption for educational charities from accounting for tax on their educational supplies under the various exemptions in Schedule 5 Group 6 Items 1 to 3.

In addition to these reliefs the Department of Customs and Excise interprets the meaning of 'supply in the course of business' so as to exclude the supply by a charity of substantially less than cost of goods or services for the relief of distress. This relieves many such charities from the obligation to register and to account for tax.

Another administrative relief relates to the position of branches of charities. Where a local branch can show that it has effective control of its own affairs and finances and its total turnover does not exceed £5,000 a year, it may be treated as a separate entity for VAT purposes and thus incur no obligation to register. Similarly where a branch is truly autonomous and is required to register by virtue of having a turnover in excess of £5,000 it can normally be registered separately without involving the head office of the charity or other branches. In addition where individuals (who may be members of the charity) organise fund raising activities in support of a charity in their own name and on their own responsibility, they are not required to register for VAT unless these (and any other business) activities are carried on by them with a turnover of more than £5,000 a year.

Duties on taxes on imported goods

Several concessions are allowed in connection with charities in the area of duties and taxes on imported goods:

(i) ... VAT ... are waived on imported articles (other than tobacco and alcoholic liquor) given or lent to non-profit-making bodies in this country, such as charitable institutions, churches, schools and social service organisations. Articles intended for sale are excluded from the waiver.

(ii) The British Red Cross are allowed to receive by gift supplies of tobacco free of ... VAT for distribution to sick or wounded serviceman and disabled ex-servicemen.

(iii) ... VAT are waived on Christmas trees ...
    (b) sent as gifts to non-profit-making organisations for public exhibition at Christmas time in connection with charitable activities

(iv) Relief is also given from ... VAT on gifts of used clothing and medical supplies imported by certain charities for sorting, repacking and re-exportation for free distribution abroad.

(v) Units of the US Air Force and Navy stationed in the UK are allowed to make gifts to charitable organisations (such as old people's homes, orphanages) from stocks of articles, new or used, which have been imported into or obtained in the UK without payment of ... VAT. The gifts must be of kind which will be used or consumed by the beneficiaries of the organisation and are not to be sold or used in any way to raise funds. Liquor and tobacco products are excluded from this concession.

9. **Rating**

The up-to-date law on rating is the General Rating Act 1967. In Section 40 of that Act relief for charities is set out. A mandatory relief of 50% is given for properties owned by, or by trustees for, a charity and wholly or mainly used for charitable purposes. Permission is given for a rating authority to grant a further 50% relief on the payment of rates chargeable on an even wider range of properties occupied by charities and non-profit-making bodies.

10. **Stamp Duty**

Under Section 49(2) of the Finance Act 1974, charities are, in relation to any conveyance, transfer or letting made or agreed to be made to them, expressly exempt from the increases in Stamp Duty specified in Schedule 11 to that Act.

Chapter VI

Registration of Charities

New Registrations

137. About 3,000 charities are registered each year at present by the Charity Commissioners. Many of these are old charities, i.e., those created before 1960. In 1975, 2,859 charities were registered, of which 2,388 were post-1960 charities. We were given a breakdown of these by the Charity Commissioners, classified according to objects, as follows:

Objects	Number
General Charitable Purposes	192
Relief of Poverty	136
Children and Young People	126
Old People	95
Health and Sickness	243
Social Welfare and Culture	572
Moral Welfare and Reform	57
Religion	133
Education	319
Misc. purposes for Benefit of the Community	74
Multiple Objects (2 or more)*	441
Total	2,388

*including many 'for general charitable purposes and in particular' . . .

The usefulness of this table in giving a picture of new trends in charities is limited. The Commissioners themselves subdivide these categories into a large number of sub-categories and some information as to trends could be gleaned from a breakdown of these sub-categories.

Modern Developments

138. Some of the more unusual types of new charities recently established according to the Commissioners have been in the field of social welfare, to meet current social problems relating to drug addiction and the consequences of the break-up of family life, and cultural matters. The formation of charities for the conservation of the environment has also become increasingly popular including, on the one hand, the prevention of pollution and, on the other, the preservation of industrial relics. Particular new developments in the charity field in the past few years have included the establishment of organisations to help battered wives and their children by providing them with alternative accommodation and in other ways; a charity for artificial kidney users; a disabled drivers' motor club; a charity for providing recorded tapes for the disabled and toy libraries.Another significant new development is the general purposes foundation or trust which collects money for distribution to other charities. Two registered in 1974 were the Charities Aid Foundation and the Charity

Stamp Fund. The less fortunate in our community remain the concern of a high proportion of the newly established charities. But the Charity Commissioners note that a changing pattern is evolving. In the past the most usual way of expressing this concern has been for people to give of their personal fortune, often by will, with instructions to trustees to apply the income for these purposes. Now there is an increasing tendency for institutions to be established with little or no permanent endowment, as a result of a small group of people joining together to pursue charitable objects which are of concern to them. The founders bring to the new charities their enthusiasm and perhaps their expertise in a particular subject, but few, or no, funds. They have to depend on the ability of the trustees to raise funds by appeals to the public or to grant-making charities or agencies. One of the fields in which this change is evident is in the number of charities for religious and social welfare purposes which are founded for immigrant communities, pioneered and administered by members of these communities themselves. These examples illustrate how charities arise to meet new needs and carry on pioneering work in fields where the welfare services do not operate or are inadequate. This is a development to be welcomed as explained in Chapter I.

Should there be restrictions on Registration?

139. Nevertheless the ever increasing level of taxation makes it a matter of concern that only charities which are serving the community in a reasonably efficient manner should enjoy the privileges which the law rightly in our view accords to charities. We therefore gave considerable thought to the question whether it should be made more difficult for organisations to be registered as charities with the prestige and fiscal advantages entailed in such registration. The Charity Commissioners had expressed a feeling that there may be some charities which benefit those who run them considerably more than the supposed beneficiaries or which simply use their resources inefficiently and ineffectively. While it is probable that there are few charities on the register which are deliberate swindles there are rather more which will eventually prove not to be very effective. They also think that perhaps too many charities are being registered and that sometimes the funds put into them would be more efficiently and economically used if channelled into existing charities. Their view is, however, that to try to limit the number of new charities registered would probably do more harm than good and that if a new charity were refused registration the resources which it would produce might not in fact be forthcoming at all. There would be a danger of stifling voluntary initiatives. In response to specific suggestions by the Committee, the Charity Commissioners thought that a power not to register similar to that exercised by the Registrar of Companies under the Companies Act, on the ground that the name was too like the name of an existing charity, or that it abused such words as 'national' or 'foundation', would be useful. On the other hand it would be difficult for them to judge at the time of registration that a charity was not likely to be properly administered, although it was recognised that, under existing law, in

the case of war charities and charities for the disabled, this type of value judgment has to be made by a local authority but the Charity Commissioners pointed out that it may be easier for a local authority to obtain the information needed to form a proper judgment than it would be for the Charity Commissioners. Whoever is responsible there are limits on the vetting that can be done without a highly organised police force established for the purpose.

Provisional Registration

140. The Charity Commissioners made a suggestion of their own that in suitable cases, they might grant a provisional registration for a period of, say, five years and at the end of that period they might have power to remove the charity from the register if it could not show that it was doing an effective job and to transfer any remaining assets to some other charity with similar objects. We feel that the proposal for provisional registration could be a most useful step. In deciding whether to grant a provisional registration or a full registration at the outset the Charity Commissioners would have to make some value judgment. At the moment of registration, there would have to be consultation between the Charity Commissioners and the trustees of the new charity on the way the charity was going to operate, so that if these doubts are not removed the registration can be made provisional. This does not seem to us to present difficulties.

Statement of Activities

141. We consider it of importance that at least in the case of charities which intend to make appeals to the public information should be available about proposed activities at the time of registration. For instance a charity generally for the relief of poverty may choose a number of different methods such as providing cash grants or direct service, encouraging self-help, undertaking community work, research, the provision of advice or even co-ordinating the work of other charities. We think that the Charity Commissioners might consider it to be desirable that they should require, when a new charity is registered, a statement in general terms of how it proposes to achieve its objects. The statement should not be incorporated into its governing instrument and would not therefore prevent it from changing its methods, but if its methods are changed it should file a supplementary statement with the Charity Commissioners which would, within reason, be made available for public inspection. If this proposal is adopted, it will assist the Charity Commissioners to compare the performance of the charity with its statement of intention when it comes to review its activities and, in conjunction with the annual report which, in a later part of this Report we suggest should accompany the statements of accounts, will make the surveillance of charities easier.

Reviews

142. On a review the Charity Commissioners should have power to make such orders as might be necessary including deregistration, the appointment of new trustees, a scheme for administering the trust or

amalgamation with existing trusts in the same field. We think that the period of five years suggested by the Charity Commissioners is too long and that the probationary period should be three years.

Scrutiny of Trustees of New Charities

143. The Committee was concerned to note that there is little or no scrutiny made of prospective charity trustees by the Charity Commissioners, either upon application for registration, or when trustees are changed. As long as the name and address of a trustee appear on a Trust Deed, little or no further evidence either of identity or suitability is required before the person is entrusted with charitable funds. The only check lies in the power of the Charity Commissioners to set up an inquiry under section 6 of the Charities Act 1960.

144. This was further highlighted by a case which received extensive publicity following a TV programme which documented a series of appalling incidents involving offences against young persons in charity hostels in the London area and suggesting that false declarations had been made when the charities were registered. This matter is now the subject of an official inquiry by the Charity Commissioners. At that time there were several calls for closer scrutiny of charity trustees made both by the media and Parliament. It does seem to us that at present it may be too easy for persons with false identities or uncharitable intentions to become trustees, although there is no evidence to suggest that such malpractices are widespread. The Committee felt that if the regular review procedure outlined earlier in this Report were put in practice and the Charity Commissioners were more diligent in their scrutiny of charitable activities, it would be possible for the opportunities for abuse to be decreased. The Committee was reluctant to suggest that charity trustees be 'vetted' prior to registration. This would not present an obstacle to determined people and would create a great deal of additional work and hard feeling if it were to be effective. It would not necessarily be desirable to bar certain categories of people with charitable intentions such as those with past criminal convictions from working in the charitable field. The Committee's attention was drawn to examples of valuable community work being undertaken by people, such as ex-offenders, who were able to draw on their own life experience. However, it should be stressed that the police and public authorities have a duty themselves to be diligent when inspecting charitable institutions and activities and should satisfy themselves when necessary of the standards of such work rather than relying merely on the existence of charitable status. It would not be practical for the Charity Commissioners to be fully knowledgeable about all staff working for charities and the public has to rely on the general protection afforded by the law. It is the case that the Charity Commissioners have power in extreme cases actually to remove trustees or staff (Charities Act 1960 Sect. 20 (1) (i)).

145. Having said this, the Committee would point out that should the recommendations made in this report result in the Charity Commission

being more well known to both trustees and the general public, it is hoped that they would be informed at an early stage if any signs of abuse are detected. Similarly, we hope that local and central government departments would be forthcoming in supplying information to the Charity Commissioners regarding the conduct of charities.

146. However, the Committee felt that there should be stricter control over applications for registration. It is essential that the Charity Commissioners should be empowered to request greater detail prior to registration and to refuse registration or intervene if this is not forthcoming or is unsatisfactory. It would not be appropriate to prescribe precise guidelines here, as, whatever is laid down, the Charity Commissioners would have to use sensitivity and discretion in seeking the appropriate information. It must be stressed that the procedure must not be so formidable that complex obstructions are placed in the way of people wishing to establish a charity. However, we consider that the Charity Commissioners must be able to satisfy themselves of the integrity of trustees and that trustees are aware of the responsibilities which they have to bear. Whilst the Committee is reluctant to suggest an elaborate vetting procedure, both for practical reasons of time and effort and for personal reasons of not wishing to deter public-spirited people it must be accepted that in the interests of public accountability some proof of integrity of trustees, many of whom will not have previous contact with the Charity Commission is required. We consider the best procedure at present to be the requirement that a declaration should be submitted containing the identity of each individual trustee, and counter-signed by two people of professional standing who have known the applicant for some period of time. The declaration would specify that there is no known reason why the applicant should not undertake responsibility for charitable funds. The form of declaration would render a signatory liable to prosecution if the information were not accurate in much the same way as in relation to an application for a passport. This would not impose an undue burden but would make people think twice before perpetrating a fraud. The Committee is satisfied that this is not a great problem, and that it is highly exceptional for such cases to arise.

We Recommend

147. **(1) That the Charity Commissioners should have power, prior to registration to require a charity to declare the name it will use and that in certain circumstances, such as a charity being established by a will, to require a name to be decided shortly after registration.**

(2) that should the full name not be declared, or should the name be misleading, or too similar to the name of an existing charity as to be confusing, or make unjustified use of currently emotive words, then the Charity Commissioners should have power to require a change in name, or to remove the charity from the register, whichever is appropriate.

(3) that any application for registration of a charity should be accompanied by a statement as to its proposed activities and methods of operation.

(4) that the Charity Commissioners should have power to require such information as they think fit about the proposed activities and having regard to the statement and any representations made by the trustees, to refuse registration if it appears appropriate or, alternatively, to grant registration subject to review after three years.

(5) that where registration has been granted subject to review, then at the end of three years the performance of the Charity should be reviewed (in relation to 3 and 4 above) and, if unsatisfied, the Charity Commissioners should intervene to effect appropriate action by the trustees. If the Charity Commissioners remain unsatisfied they should take the action which they are presently empowered to do by appointing new trustees; or should have power to establish a scheme for administering the trust, or amalgamate with existing trustees in the same field, or remove the charity from the register, whichever is appropriate.

(6) that the Charity Commissioners have power to require certain detailed information about trustees either prior to or after registration, and satisfy themselves of the accuracy of this information and the integrity of trustees. But that these procedures should not necessarily preclude ex-offenders and similar people from working in the charitable field. Such procedures should be kept under review by the Charity Commissioners.

(7) that a charity should be legally obliged to inform the Charity Commissioners of any changes in the information declared relating to names and addresses of trustees or the activities of the trust.

(8) that the Charity Commissioners should be empowered to refuse registration of a charity or intervene in the case of an existing charity where these procedures are not complied with.

It should be emphasised that there is no desire to stifle a variety of approaches in the name of administrative tidiness.

Registration Procedures

148. The procedure for registering a charity is fairly informal at present. Frequently a person or body wishing to set up a charity will prepare a draft in consultation with a Solicitor or with some other adviser and submit it to the Charity Commissioners. If there are difficulties the Charity Commissioners may make written comments and a meeting may take place where suggestions can be canvassed to achieve a satisfactory solution. In many other cases the person proposing to set up a charity will consult the Commissioners at the outset and they will help to draft the objects of the trust to ensure that they are charitable and that the administrative provisions of the trust deed are appropriate. Sometimes a trust has already been set up and referred to the Charity Commissioners as a *fait accompli* and if there is

any difficulty it may be necessary to unscramble it. In the vast majority of cases there is no difficulty in achieving registration by these methods. However, when the Charity Commissioners are inclined to refuse an application they sit as a Board to reach a final decision in a formal way. For this reason the Commissioners do not personally deal with applications until this formal stage. This we feel may result in their not being fully aware of the lines which their junior staff are adopting. That staff is usually in close contact with the Inland Revenue and it has been suggested to us that as a result in some cases the opinions issuing from the Charity Commissioners may reflect the views of the Inland Revenue rather than those of the Commissioners themselves. The Commissioners do not accept this. We think that in any event it should be made clear to the public that the ultimate arbiters are the Charity Commissioners and not their staff and that they should publish regularly and systematically summaries of examples of their decisions and of the way in which they administer the law in addition to those already given in their annual report.

Role of the Inland Revenue

149. In some cases the Charity Commissioners may deem it necessary to consult the Inland Revenue. This they have power to do under Section 9 of the Charities Act 1960. They do not do so in what they consider to be non-contentious cases. If they think that some amendment is necessary a copy is sent to the Inland Revenue and usually a joint opinion of the Charity Commissioners and Inland Revenue is sent to the applicant. Where the draft is considered unacceptable and the Commissioners think that the Inland Revenue may have some background information the Commissioners invite comment from the Inland Revenue. Where the Commissioners are satisfied that the objects are not charitable they so inform the applicant without consulting the Inland Revenue. There is a similar liaison where an executed instrument is submitted for registration. The Commissioners inform us that there is rarely disagreement between them and the Inland Revenue but in some cases where the Commissioners are inclined to accept an application the Inland Revenue will consult their own lawyers and may submit a formal Memorandum of Objection. The applicant is usually supplied with a copy and his comments invited. Then the Charity Commissioners decide the issue as a Board. But that is not the end. The Inland Revenue as an interested party may appeal to the High Court against acceptance just as the applicant may appeal against a rejection. And even after registration the Revenue may refuse tax relief if it claims that the income of a charity is not being applied for charitable purposes only. The Inland Revenue may thus exercise a more effective invigilation role over the activities of a charity than the Charity Commissioners. It may, for instance, raise a query if a charity is accumulating its income rather than expending it, although if there is a legitimate reason for accumulation relief will be allowed. Because its proceedings are confidential, it does not inform the Charity Commissioners if it disallows expenditure.

150. The present procedures have been criticised on a number of grounds. It is said that it is difficult to find out the interpretation put on 'charity' by the Charity Commissioners in accepting or refusing applications and that their proceedings should be more open; that the dual role of the Charity Commissioners and Inland Revenue in relation to the registration and subsequent surveillance of the activities of charities is objectionable; and that the cost of appealing to the High Court against a refusal is prohibitive.

Appeals

151. It would not be a useful exercise in our view to make every application for registration the subject of a formal public hearing. The informal procedures outlined above work well in the vast majority of cases. In these there is no dispute between the Commissioners and the Inland Revenue. What then of the difficult cases? The difficulty may be in deciding (a) whether as a matter of law the objects are charitable; or (b) if our proposals for review of registration (and in exceptional cases refusal of registration) are accepted whether registration is appropriate having regard to the way that the charity is being run or likely to be run.

(a) Suggestions have been made that appeals on the issue of whether the objects are charitable should be made to a tribunal rather than to the High Court to save expense. This would only make sense if the decision of the tribunal although only on a point of law, was final. We consider that on points of law the High Court should be the final arbiter. But the expense of an appeal is such that, if the High Court is appropriate there should be provision for organisations to be granted legal aid under the existing Legal Aid Scheme suitably adapted to accommodate appeals from organisations.

(b) We consider that appeals from the administrative decisions of the Charity Commissioners should be made to an appellate tribunal only the chairman of which should be legally qualified and before whom appellants might conduct their cases in person or with the help of a friend or legal adviser. There would always be a right of appeal from this Tribunal on points of law.

152. Is there any role for the Inland Revenue to play in the registration procedure? We heard powerful arguments to the contrary but since the Charity Commissioners in registering a charity perform a quasi judicial function it is of benefit that there should be a body which in appropriate cases can argue the case against registration, and since the charity, if registered, will have fiscal reliefs, it seems proper that the Revenue should have a *locus standi* in an appeal. Equally, after a charity has been registered, the decision whether any income or expenditure qualifies for relief against taxation is best dealt with through the ordinary Inland Revenue channels. If this function were transferred to the Charity Commissioners, their staff would have to be greatly increased to allow them not only to check a great many more accounts but also to maintain an adequate intelligence service. A suggestion was made that it would be sufficient if charity accounts had all to be audited (as later

recommended in this Report) and if auditors had to certify that all the income had been applied for charitable purposes. Such a certificate by professional accountants might normally obviate the necessity for further checks, but it would still be necessary to exercise a long-stop vigilance and it seems reasonable to leave this function to the Inland Revenue. The Charity Commissioners look at accounts for different purposes which are summarised later in this Report, so that the argument against two bodies looking at the same set of accounts is not really valid. This again is a difficult question but on the whole we think the dual function of the Revenue and the Commission should continue.

The Effect of Registration

153. Under Section 5(1) of the Charities Act 1960, registration raises a conclusive presumption that an institution is a charity as long as it is on the register. There is no converse proposition that absence of registration is conclusive evidence against charitable status. It would seem that there may be many 'old' charities i.e. pre-1960 charities, still not registered though this ought not to be the case 16 years after the Act was passed. It seems reasonable that in order to gain the privileges of a charity, an institution should at least have to have applied for registration. If registration is refused, or if no application is made, that should preclude it from all fiscal benefits unless it is exempt or excepted from registration (in which case it should obtain a certificate that it is an exempted or excepted charity). If an application has been made and subsequently succeeds then fiscal benefits could date from the date of the application.

We Recommend:

154. **(a) That the existing Legal Aid Scheme suitably adapted should be available to organisations wishing to appeal from the decisions of the Charity Commissioners on points of law.**

(b) appeals from the administrative decisions of the Charity Commissioners should be made to an appellate tribunal. There should be a right of appeal to the courts from decisions of this tribunal on points of law.

(c) that the Inland Revenue should continue to exercise its existing functions in matters relating to registration and administration of tax relief.

(d) that no fiscal benefits should accrue to a charity (other than an exempted or excepted charity) until it has made an application for registration after which it may be granted provisional benefits until the decision. Where registration is refused or cancelled this should preclude fiscal benefits.

Exempted and Excepted Charities

155. Criticisms have been made of the exemption of charities and of the exceptions made in the requirement to submit accounts. 'Exemption' means that a charity need not register or submit accounts to the Charity Commission. It is not however entirely outside the

jurisdiction of the Charity Commissioners. 'Excepted' charities may be excused from registering or from submitting accounts other than on request or from getting permission to dispose of their permanent endowment, or a combination of these. The exemptions include universities and colleges. They account to the University Grants Committee so there it may be thought that there is no special reason why the Charity Commission should have the task of looking over their accounts also. Other exempted bodies are registered industrial, provident and friendly societies which have their own Registrar, certain museums, some ecclesiastical funds exempted before the 1960 Act and the Church Commissioners and any institution administered by them. Unless very much wider forms of control are to be given to the Charity Commission, it seems that only dogmatic insistence on uniformity would justify adding to useless paperwork by removing those exemptions. The 'exceptions' include some voluntary schools, small funds of Boy Scouts and Girl Guides, various forms of religious charities. In some cases of this sort blanket registration by the parent body, which includes the branches in its filed annual report, provides the solution. Charities administered by hospital boards, Area Health Authorities, or hospital management boards, and some service charities are also excepted. No charity is required to register in respect of any place of worship registered under Section 9 of the Places of Worship Registration Act 1855. The philosophy behind some of these exceptions is by no means so clear and the validity of the exemptions and exceptions should be reviewed. We have not ourselves had sufficient evidence on this subject.

By the Act itself a charity having neither a permanent endowment nor income from property exceeding £15 a year nor occupation of any land need not register. There seems to be very little logic in this since theoretically at least a charity might have a very large turnover without being required to register.

Effect of Exemptions and Exceptions

156. What other effects do exemptions and exceptions have? On its terms the general functions given by Section 1 of the Act to the Charity Commissioners to promote efficiency, to give advice and check abuses apply to all charities. 'Exempt' charities cannot be the subject of inquiries, individually or as a class, under Section 6. The Charity Commissioners cannot call for the documents of an 'exempt' charity under Section 7. The powers of making schemes and applying property *cy-pres* can be exercised in respect of exempt charities, but the compulsory powers where the trustees do not consent do not apply to exempt charities. The costs of promoting a Bill in Parliament can in the case of an exempt charity be paid out of charitable funds without the consent of the Court or the Commissioners. Orders for the removal of a trustee cannot be made as the result of an inquiry under Section 6, since such inquiries do not apply to exempt charities but the Commissioners can replace a trustee of an exempt charity if the trustee is bankrupt or mentally incapable, refuses to act or is abroad or cannot be traced.

Common investment funds, of which all the participating charities are exempt charities, are themselves exempt charities.

The miscellaneous powers of the Commissioners under sections 24 to 27 do apply to exempt charities. An exempt charity can institute charity proceedings without the consent of the Commissioners and can likewise dispose of property forming part of its permanent endowment. The power of the Attorney-General to petition for the winding-up of a charitable company applies to exempt charities. The general duty to keep proper accounts likewise applies.

The special provisions summarised above in relation to 'exempt' charities do not apply to 'excepted' charities which are excepted only to the extent specified in the order or regulation excepting them.

Conclusions and Recommendations

157. We have not had any evidence suggesting that the statutory exemptions and exceptions give rise to any abuse but we think that the validity of some of them should be re-examined. There is a feeling that somewhere should be available a complete picture of charities in the country. We do not see the justification for Section 4(4) (c), of the Charities Act 1960; accordingly, **WE RECOMMEND that the freedom from registration given by the Act to charities having neither a permanent endowment nor income from property exceeding £15 nor occupation of any land should be removed, and that the Home Secretary should re-examine regularly the validity of the other classes of exemptions and exceptions.**

Constitution of Charities

In connection with registration of new charities we have had evidence from various sources about the constitution of charities including suggestions of model deeds. We consider a few of the points below.

158. (i) **Company, Trust or Unincorporated Association**

Charities may be formed as companies limited by guarantee, as trusts, as unincorporated associations or occasionally by royal charter. According to the Charity Commissioners, when we saw them, the form which the constitution of a charity takes is usually governed by the whim of the solicitor who advises on its formation. We had conflicting evidence about this. It has been suggested on the one hand that to have a company structure means that there is a dual control since the company has to conform with the provisions of the Companies Acts and also with the requirements of the Charity Commissioners. On the other hand, it has been suggested that in the case of large charities it is a good thing that they should be incorporated under the Companies Acts so that the stringent provisions as to accounts and administration which are contained in the Companies Acts should apply to them in full, in addition to the less stringent requirements of the Charities Act.

We do not think that it is possible to lay down a hard and fast rule having regard to the great variety of charities which exist. A company structure may be appropriate in some cases in that it has the advantage of limiting the liability of the directors. An unincorporated association may be appropriate where the charity is formed by a large number of people who wish to be associated in its running. There are difficulties about an unincorporated association in the questions of how far its members can benefit and who is responsible for its management, although these can be obviated by a well drawn constitution.

159. (ii) **Rotation of Trustees: Position of Trustees and Employees**

We have had a great many suggestions that there should be provision for the retirement of trustees by rotation after a certain number of years and that they should not be self-perpetuating bodies. Here again, it is difficult to lay down a hard and fast rule. The Charity Commissioners take a different attitude to endowments by a single donor who has within reason a power to dictate the structure of the charity which is being created with his money, as opposed to a case where there is an intention to make appeals to the public. In the latter case there may be much stronger arguments for saying that the trustees should not be in the gift of the donor and that there should be on occasion some representative of the public among the trustees. Also that there should be a regular system of replacement of trustees or re-election of trustees at regular intervals.

160. (iii) **Age Limits**

There have been persistent suggestions that there should be a provision for an age of retirement and it is undoubtedly the fact that there are many trustees of charities who are very old and who resist any form of change and it is an embarrassing exercise for their co-trustees to try to ease them away from their position of responsibility. We think that an age for retirement of trustees other than ex officio trustees should be fixed at 70. We think this rule should immediately apply to all new trustees and should be brought in in respect of existing charities after a short interval.

These are certainly matters which should be taken into consideration at the time of registration of a charity, or at the time when a scheme is made. Perhaps the Charities Board which we recommend later could help the Charity Commissioners to reach decisions on the constitution of a charity which has applied for registration and we think that even if the charity is one created by the founder which does not intend to make appeals to the public, the Charity Commissioners should take a fairly firm stand on the questions of the constitution of the charity as regards the appointment and re-election of trustees.

161. (iv) **Benefits to Trustees**

Another matter which has been raised in this connection is the extent to which trustees should have power to receive appropriate benefits from the trust. The Commissioners again take a slightly different view in the case of an endowment founded by a single donor and a charity which is going to appeal to the public. In the former case, if the donor wishes to provide that trustees in appropriate cases may take some remuneration, then they may be prepared to allow this but they take a much stricter view if appeals are to be made to the public, and by and large this seems to us to be right. However, in companies, senior executives are very often appointed to the board and an argument can be made that the person who perhaps has devoted his life as a chief executive to building up a charity should be entitled to be involved in the decision making process. An obvious example is the artistic director of a subsidised charitable theatre company. It has been suggested that it is invidious that he should be completely debarred from being a member of the council of the theatre and it may well be desirable that playwrights, actors and others who might from time to time either have plays put on at the theatre or act in such plays should nevertheless be members of the council, bringing to it their expert knowledge and experience. Equally it is important to prevent abuse by the setting up of charities, the main purpose of which is to provide an income for those employed by the charity and this is a matter which would be considered upon the review of new charities and as part of the examination of accounts by the Charity Commissioners. It is possible for such people to attend meetings as advisers and exert considerable influence.

162. A similar problem relates to self-help organisations, which have been considered in Chapter II para. 45. If these are to be allowed in appropriate cases a charitable status, then it is clear that the trustees must in such cases be members of the organisation who in common with others may benefit from the charitable trust. There is authority for the proposition that charitable status is not necessarily endangered if the members of the society have some incidental benefits provided that they are small in relation to the charitable purposes.

We Recommend

163. **(a) that all charities should normally have in their trust instrument a provision for rotation of trustees other than ex officio trustees;**

(b) that there should be an age limit of 70 for trustees, other than ex officio trustees;

(c) that these provisions should apply immediately to new trustees and to existing trustees after three years;

(d) that the position should be reviewed from time to time by the Charities Board that we have recommended;

(e) that in order to ensure that the charity is not just a means of providing an income for the executives they should not be trustees even in charities in specialised fields such as the arts but that the Charity Commissioners should have power to waive this rule in special cases.

Employees of Charities

164. The question has been raised in evidence whether it is proper for

charities to make *ex gratia* payments to ex-employees in circumstances where any other responsible employer might feel a moral duty to do so. If there is indeed any doubt about this then it should be made clear that such payments are as proper in the case of a charity as they would be in the case of any other employer.

Disaster Funds

165. There have been various suggestions that disaster funds give rise to special problems. They often have to be set up fairly rapidly to deal with an emergency situation. The two problems which most frequently arise result –

(a) from more than one fund being set up at the same time, and

(b) from the amount of money subscribed being either more or less than is required for the situation.

166. As regards such funds, the Charity Commissioners should, we think, be given power to decide between the funds and to make necessary arrangements for amalgamating them. The problem of over and under-subscription is not confined to disasters. It may apply to an appeal launched for any specific project such as the repair of a cathedral, the erection of a statue to a prominent citizen who has died, or some other form of memorial. The important thing in these cases is that the trust deed should provide for these contingencies. Appeals to the public should make clear how the money is to be used in these contingencies. The Charity Commisioners should have a model trust deed to meet cases of this sort so that registration could be effected speedily and without such formality. The Charities Board which we recommend later in this Report might in some cases have a function in assisting the Charity Commissioners to decide between one fund and another and in suggesting what is to happen to surplus moneys or if too little is provided.

We Recommend

167. **(a) the Charity Commissioners should be given power to decide between such funds whether any arrangements are necessary for amalgamating these funds as may be desirable;**

(b) the trust deed should always state explicitly what is to happen in the event of over-subscription or under-subscription;

(c) the Charity Commissioners should have available a model trust deed to facilitate speedy registration; and

(d) in questions arising relating to such funds the Charity Commissioners should have the assistance of the Charities Board.

Registration Fee

168. There has been a suggestion from several quarters that charities should be required to pay a registration fee, either on registration or annually or both. It is suggested that since no money will be available for the time being to implement the recommendations of this Commitee

in so far as they involve additional expenditure, a registration fee would help to provide the necessary funds. It has also been suggested as a method of putting pressure on small charities to amalgamate and rationalise themselves so that they will be able to pay a registration fee. It must, however, be borne in mind that charities are very hard hit by inflation at the present time and that whatever money is taken away from them by way of registration fee or otherwise will reduce the total amount of money available for charitable purposes. It is clear that the process of amalgamation of small charities is bound to be a fairly slow process and all witnesses on this subject have explained the initial resistance which has to be overcome. We do not think that the imposition of a registration fee which might exceed the income of many of these small charities is the proper way to put pressure upon them. Indeed we are not enamoured of the idea of any registration fee.

We Recommend

169. **that there should be no registration fee.**

Chapter VII

Administration and Surveillance of Charities

Part I – Introduction

Importance of Good Administration

170. That charities should be administered efficiently is a matter of importance. If they are to be given financial privileges, then the community is entitled to be sure that their resources are being put to the best possible use in the service of the community. The public who respond to appeals made by charities, who give their time or support should be able to have full confidence that the money and effort is put to a proper use. At the same time it is important not to discourage charitable impulses by too much regimentation or to increase the administration expenses of charities beyond what is necessary at the expense of the funds available for the charitable work, there being no evidence whatsoever of widespread abuse.

171. The problem is complicated by the enormous differences in the size of charities and in their structure and functions. There are as will be seen a very great many small charities with an income which is individually insignificant but which in aggregate amounts to a very considerable sum. At the other end of the scale are large charities whose income runs into seven figures and in between there are charities of all sizes. There are those, which rely entirely on their original capital left in perpetuity by will or trust, those which rely almost entirely for their income from responses to appeals to the public, and those which have large capital assets supplemented by appeals and collections. There are those which provide a service themselves and those that hand out money to other charities to provide the service. Fund-raising methods used by collecting charities are infinitely varied, ranging from appeals by circular or through the media, through football pools, lotteries, fetes, balls, to sponsored walks, and collections of milk bottle tops. New methods are always being thought up by keen fund raisers.

172. Statutory provisions governing registration and accountability of charities have grown up in a rather haphazard piecemeal fashion. The main provisions are contained in the Charities Act 1960. In addition war charities and charities for the disabled have to register with the appropriate local authority and charities organising house-to-house collections or street collections have to register under two separate Acts and render accounts to separate authorities. Apart from these provisions it is possible for a charity to register with the Charity Commissioners and to appeal to the public.

173. In the following section we shall look into the law relating to: co-ordination and rationalisation of existing local charities and the larger national ones; into methods of fund raising; the surveillance and accountability of charities; the provision of a service of advice, both to charities and to the public; and a number of problems which have been brought to our notice in the course of the inquiry relating to the administration of charities.

Part II – Review and Co-Ordination of Local Charities

The Present Position

174. The Nathan Committee attached great value to a partnership between local charities and public social services and urged that powers of scheme-making should be used to ensure that charity trustees put their resources to the best possible use in the service of the community. For this purpose, the Charities Act 1960 gave powers to local authorities to maintain an index of local charities and to initiate and carry out a review of the working of any group of local charities with the same or similar purposes in the council's area. This review could only be carried out, however, with the consent of the trustees of the charity to be reviewed. However, the purposes of such a review are nowhere defined by statute, although the Charity Commissioners have from time to time produced basic guidelines for review organisers, have held meetings with review organisers, given individual advice, and made reports of general progress of reviews and items of specific interest in their annual reports to Parliament. Local authorities could also make arrangements for co-ordinating the activities of the authority with those of the charity in the interests of persons who might benefit from the services or from the charity. And the Charity Commissioners could use their powers of making schemes and *cy-pres* orders to further this process. It is a feature of the legislation prescribing the functions of local government that the authorities are empowered to carry out many functions in co-operation with, or totally by, voluntary organisations. This also includes the provision of grant aid to, and facilities for, voluntary organisations. However, local authorities have no power in law to use any method other than persuasion to gain the co-operation of charity trustees in any suggestions relating to the activities or conduct of the charity. One of the tasks which we undertook was to try to make some assessment of how these powers relating to the conduct of charity reviews were working, and what had been achieved 16 years after the passing of the Act. We are informed that, at the time of writing this Report, some 48 reviews have been undertaken, very often confined to charities for the relief of poverty in a parish. The reviews conducted to date have thus focused mainly on endowed trusts, usually for parish poor. Where wider groups of charities have been included in the review, endowed funds have been examined rather than service providing charities. No local authority, to our knowledge, has made a comprehensive review of all the various types of charity and their numerous activities. Of these 48 reviews 16 have been completed. We studied in detail the reports of three reviews, representing differing

viewpoints. From these we obtained a vivid picture of the enormous number of small charities involved over the country as a whole. Although many of these charities have microscopic incomes, the total sum involved is quite significant – probably £3-4 million in all – and the total amount in relief against taxation is correspondingly significant, though not in comparison to the large charities.

The Case for Compulsion

175. In one county which we studied, the total number of parish charities for the relief of poverty was 365, with a total income of £13,249 at the time when the review was undertaken, and 157 out of the 365 charities had an income of less than £5 per annum. The result of the review in co-ordinating these charities and in helping them to invest their funds more profitably was to reduce the total number of charities from 365 to 216 and to increase their total income from £13,249 to £17,943. Another factor which was noticed was that there were some parishes with no charities and other parishes which had six or more overlapping charities. The number of charities and their income bore no relation to the population of the parishes or their needs. One parish, for instance, with a population of 11,000 had four charities with a total income of £8; another parish with a population of 600 had a total income from one charity of £280. Many of the charities were restricted by their terms to a particular kind of benefit or a particular class of poor person, restrictions which were quite unsuitable if the charity were effectively to fulfil its objects in present-day society. Most of the money was found to be given away only in small more or less equal amounts at Christmas to the same people year after year. The Review Officer's principal aims were to encourage trustees to come together in groups of parishes or at least to merge all charities found in a single parish; to apply for removal of restrictions which prevented them from providing whatever was needed to anyone in need; to review investments and to make contact with welfare workers. He had a fair amount of success in merging charities within parishes but found it almost impossible to group charities in different parishes or promote co-operation with welfare workers. He felt that he did not have sufficient support from the Charity Commissioners who refused two applications for grouping of parishes, although one, after strong protest, was subsequently allowed. He formed the impression that the Charity Commissioners' original policy of merging parish charities for the poor had been abandoned in favour of a policy of diverting the income of large charities to other purposes than relief in order to keep the charity within the parish and he claimed that this reversal of policy had the effect that the social aims of the Charities Act are virtually ignored and that, in addition, each charity is looked at separately and not in relation either to others or to the social services. He was in favour of promotion with a measure of compulsion of the 'Neighbourhood Trust' as a means by which parish charities could be restored to the field of genuine welfare but he pointed out that the formation of 'Neighbourhood Trusts' requires the active co-operation and support of the Charity Commissioners and this, he

complained, was not forthcoming. These various criticisms have been vigorously denied by the Charity Commissioners.

176. A working party subsequently set up in this county reported enthusiastically in favour of setting up 'Neighbourhood Trusts' to absorb the small parish charities and create a fund which could make a real contribution to welfare. They suggested that these 'Neighbourhood Trusts' should be organised with boundaries coinciding with petty sessional divisions and envisaged their providing for needs of the following kinds:-

(a) helping the many people in pressing financial and material need who have to be refused help by the statutory services either because their particular circumstances do not precisely meet the tests laid down in the legislation; or because the statutory authority concerned cannot meet all entitlements out of its budget.

(b) providing help designed to prevent people from becoming a charge on statutory funds, e.g. children from being taken into care, the elderly into old people's homes, the overtired from becoming hospital cases.

(c) helping with the cost of travelling expenses, particularly for hospital visiting, the cost of which is now so high that from rural areas particularly and even to children it is becoming increasingly difficult and restricted.

(d) helping with petrol or mileage allowances to make it possible for voluntary associations to continue the services they provide which the current cost of petrol makes increasingly difficult to do.

(e) supporting play groups, day centres, old people's clubs.

The working party suggested legislation which would have the desired effect, either immediately or after a period during which parish trustees would be invited to make suitable alternative proposals. They thought that trusts on this scale might attract donations and bequests in a way in which parish charities have been unable to do. Such an amalgamation, it is suggested, would reduce the time at present spent by all concerned in finding sources of financial and material help and could better facilitate the exchange and collection of information about new needs as they develop, between the charities.

The Case For Persuasion

177. Another Review Organiser took a very different standpoint regarding reviews although he found a very similar situation at the outset. He found that the review was welcomed by the vast majority of trustees, although in a few cases resentment was shown at being approached by anyone other than the Charity Commissioners. The organiser acknowledged the encouragement and support of the Charity Commissioners, the local authority and others. But he found very limited support for any suggestion that one parish might unite its charities for the poor with those of another parish although he found instances of one parish amalgamating with a poorer neighbour. He felt

that this less parochial attitude would increase. He persuaded his Council to extend the review procedure to educational, apprenticeship and almshouse charities. In a memorandum to the committee, he emphasised the point that a grouping of charities in several parishes, although possibly desirable, was not the yardstick by which the success of the review was to be measured. The maintenance of a local index of charities, the encouragement of co-operation within parishes and, above all, the liaison between charities and the welfare services seem to him to be the most important objects of a review. He had brought the existence of charitable funds to the notice of welfare officers who in turn could refer to trustees cases of real need. We also received evidence of the working within a parish of two charities, one for the relief of the poor and one educational, for the benefit of the inhabitants of a rural parish of between 5,000 and 7,000 inhabitants. The charity for the relief of the poor was already a united charity set up when three parishes had been amalgamated. Its objects had included a supply of gowns for maidens and a scheme had been obtained modernising the objects. For many years the income, which amounted to about £92 per annum, had been divided between the incumbents of the three parishes and distributed to the same families year after year. As a result of the review great care was now taken to see that the funds were distributed where they could do most good. Doctors, nurses and welfare workers were consulted and the money was never used for purposes which could be served by the welfare services; for instance, an appeal for blankets was referred to the W.R.V.S and no help was given with the rent of council houses; but the fund had borne the cost of a free holiday for a widow and of household equipment for another family which could not afford it. It became clear that if the work of discovering need and deciding how to distribute funds were costed, the sums which would be charged would more than exhaust the fund. Nevertheless, everyone felt that a useful service was being done. The educational charity was an amalgamation of three funds, an original educational foundation, an apprenticeship trust to provide £10 for tools and another small gift to provide a medal or prize in a local school, the income of which was only 50p. These three charities were amalgamated under a scheme as a result of the review. Their total income was about £170 and the sort of thing on which the money was spent was enabling children, whose parents could not afford it, to go on school educational visits or tours. Some apprenticeships had also been arranged and money for books provided.

178. Taking the county as a whole, at a rough estimate there might be some 1,200 trustees involved in administering the various charities. There was a total income of £41,000 as regards charities for the poor and £32,000 as regards educational charities. The trustees of which all gave dedicated services free of charge. The review of charities for the poor and sick had taken five years, the review of educational charities another two years. Probably it could not have been done any faster, as there was a lot of suspicion to overcome, suspicion particularly that the review was a prelude to some kind of state takeover. The accounts of all

these charities were submitted to and examined by parish councils, care always being taken to see that the names of the recipients were not disclosed. The Review Officer was very insistent that a continuing service of some sort was vital. The review had awakened lively interest in the need for co-operation with the welfare authority and for the best use of the funds of the charities although it was felt new trustees would take over and new welfare officers and things would probably slip back to where they were. The Review Officer had persuaded the council to employ someone once a week and also the Charity Commissioners, to visit the county for a week every three or four years to meet trustees. He had found the Charity Commissioners helpful, although there had been disagreements with them and there were complaints that they were slow in replying to letters. Their pamphlets were good but written in 'London Language'. Asked about new charities being created in the area, he mentioned one very successful one to teach the disabled to fish, special chairs and equipment being provided from funds raised for the purpose.

Inclosure Trusts

179. A difference of opinion between the two counties given as examples above which arouses strong feeling locally lies in the way in which Inclosure Trusts should be dealt with. One argues that these trusts were created by statute to compensate villagers for the loss of rights in the common land of the villages and that they should be used to provide amenities for the villagers concerned and they disagree with the Charity Commissioners that such trusts must be used for the relief of individual poverty. It would like to see legislation expressly supporting their point of view. The other would object to any compulsion in this direction, leaving it to the Charity Commission to consider each case on its merits, taking into consideration the views of the local inhabitants as well as those of the trustees. On the whole we support the latter view.

A Third Example

180. The third Review which we studied related to a Midland city well endowed with charities. The director reported some initial difficulty in getting co-operation but nevertheless he does appear to have succeeded in the end in creating a better spirit and in achieving some amalgamations of small charities. The interesting point is that the review was not confined to charities for the poor. The director encouraged co-operation between the welfare services and charities providing homes for the aged, and was able in one or two cases to arrange for homes threatened with closure to be kept open. There was also co-operation in respect of hostels and homes providing temporary shelter during rehabilitation periods. Here the charities were able to concentrate on specialist types of accommodation, such as homes for mothers who could not cope with their difficulties or had been placed on probation for child neglect. The existence of such homes is of great importance to the public services and, although theoretically the cost should all be borne by the public, charities provide much voluntary

manpower and some contribution to the cost in instances where the public services are regrettably inadequate. The same applies to accommodation for ex-prisoners and persons of no fixed abode. In the sphere of health and medicine the director found much pioneer work being done by charities in connection with alcoholics and drug addicts, advice on contraception and abortion and help to the mentally handicapped. He found that, if anything, there were too many charities catering for children and young persons in the area, though we do not think that this is a universal experience in the country as a whole. The review director was able to point to co-operation in respect of a purpose built school for autistic children, the city providing the site and the education department providing specialist staff for the school when built. Like other review organisers, he suggested that a permanent organisation should be set up to assist charities, the public welfare services and the individual and to carry on the work of co-operation initiated by the review. The review director also recommended that a reconstructed Charity Commission should maintain a local representative in large cities to advise on grouping, amalgamations and new objects and in general to assist any charity at any time. This particular review also included a study of Community Chests and Common Good Funds by a small committee. It concluded that, on the whole, it would be unlikely that a Community Chest as such would be welcomed at the present time. So far as concerns collecting charities, there was a feeling that they could individually raise more *in toto* than a Community Chest.

Views of Charity Commissioners

181. We put to the Charity Commissioners the conflicting opinions expressed by the review officers and the suggestion that the Charity Commissioners unduly restricted themselves by the principles which they applied. In reply they emphasised the point that amalgamation is not as important as working in consultation. They claim that they keep their approach to local reviews as flexible as possible. They did not accept that they had adopted the restrictive principles attributed to them and they pointed out that the *cy-pres* rule had in any event certain limitations. They say that they have been asked in the case of charities for the poor and for the sick to remove old trust limitations and substitute new wider objects enabling trustees to exercise ingenuity and imagination in putting their resources to good use. They have produced leaflets from time to time for the guidance of organisers of local reviews and they say that many modernised trusts have emerged as a result of the reviews; that there is a far greater awareness of local welfare facilities and shortcomings and that a large number of bodies of trustees have revised their methods of administration and the distribution of their income. Reviews did not start until 1966, since first priority was given to central registration. The way things were going the Commissioners thought reviews would take a century to complete. The Charity Commissioners had done a pilot review of their own unofficially in Preston and found this more successful than the reviews set up by local authorities. They did not themselves put in an appearance

normally in the course of local reviews, although they were available for advice. They thought, unless their advice was asked for or they were invited to make schemes, they were probably not welcome but their staff did from time to time make visits to places in the country. They agreed that it was necessary to see that once a review had been done the good work was kept up. They made one suggestion of their own regarding the problem of small local endowed charities and that was that they might be permitted to spend their capital. If they spent the whole of their capital, this would, of course, result in their disappearance.

Views of Local Authorities

182. We also discussed the questions of co-operation and of reviews with representatives of the Association of District Councils and the Association of Metropolitan Authorities. They explained to us that local authorities had been in the throes of reorganisation for some time and this was one of the reasons for their inability to give a great deal of attention to co-operation and reviews. They also agreed that they had to overcome considerable distrust on the part of local charities and they felt reviews were best carried out under the auspices of a local council for voluntary service which should be financed partly by the Charity Commissioners and partly by the local authority. The question of co-ordinating all these very large numbers of local endowed trusts was a mammoth task and it was sometimes doubtful whether the end product justified the effort. They felt that, while the new authorities would complete reviews already in progress, in present financial circumstances, they are not likely to expend money on new reviews. We asked them whether the local index prepared in accordance with the Charities Act were of great use and consulted. Their belief was that the public did not consult the index, which in any case did not give a great deal of information, but social workers did consult the index and make themselves familiar with local charities and copies of the index were often held by local councils for voluntary service, who would also know a good deal more about the charity. A further reason for little reference being made to the index could be that in most areas comprehensive lists of useful names and addresses of charities and associated voluntary organisations are compiled and maintained by the Council for Voluntary Service or Community Council, and further information about specific trust funds may be kept by the leading local charities or Citizens Advice Bureaux.

Neighbourhood Trusts

183. There has been a good deal of reference in the evidence to Neighbourhood Trusts, Community Trusts or Common Good Funds. We prefer to use the words Neighbourhood Trusts which we take to be a trust for the benefit of the inhabitants of a given area. The objects of the trust would cover all the heads of charity, relief of poverty, education, religion and public good such as amenities, recreation, etc., and the trustees would be recruited from public-spirited citizens in the area. It would be entirely independent of any local or public authority, though

representatives of these bodies might be included among the trustees.

Conclusions

184. The impression we get from these varied review reports and the other evidence is that the review procedure can perform and in many cases, is performing a useful service as regards local endowed charities in promoting co-operation among charities and between charities and the public services and that this work should be continued as speedily as possible. The review director often has to contend with intense initial suspicion that the object of the exercise is a takeover by the local authority or the body conducting the review on its behalf such as the Community Council. The review works best when it is carried out under the auspices of a Council for Voluntary Service or a Community Council or other local voluntary body. There does seem to be a strong current of opinion emerging from all the reviews that while they are in progress, active support and encouragement should be given on the spot by a representive of the Charity Commissioners and their advice and encouragement would contribute greatly to the success of the process. It is also clear that much will remain to be done when the review has been completed to ensure that co-operation among local endowed charities and between them and the public services continues to be fostered.

185. We are disappointed that after 16 years comparatively little progress has been made in dealing with the problem of the small endowed charities and one can understand the suggestion which has been made to us from several sources that compulsory powers should be used to compel amalgamation of charities whose funds are so small as to prevent them from making a useful contribution to the welfare of their area. The administration of some of them, it is said, is in the hands of elderly trustees who resist change and who do not even know the source of income of the trust and sometimes have stock certificates in the names of people long dead. On the other hand, many of these charities are ancient. They cost the country nothing in the sense that the services of the trustees are given free of charge and in most cases with a genuine desire to do the most good with the money available. The comparative lack of success of reviews has been due, in our view, to a number of factors. Many local authorities who are charged with the conduct of local reviews are too busy particularly following reorganisation to take much interest. The Charity Commissioners have taken the view that they should not themselves intervene except where their advice is specifically sought or if they are asked to make schemes while the review officers and trustees on their side sometimes complain of the lack of interest by the Charity Commissioners. On the whole we think that the solution, at any rate for the next ten years or so, lies not in compulsion but in a more enthusiastic form of persuasion. We think that the idea of collecting the small charities together into Neighbourhood Trusts is a good one. It would make administration much easier. It would enable the welfare services to have access to funds of reasonable size to cover cases where the public services do not

apply or are inadequate for one good reason or another. It would be most important, in our view, that any such fund should be entirely independent of central or local government control and no doubt it could invite the services of the trustees of trusts which were amalgamated in the Neighbourhood Trust. To preserve this independence and having regard to the lack of interest on the part of many local authorities we feel that the whole review procedure should now be directed by representatives of the Charity Commissioners assisted by the local voluntary services and then on completion some permanent arrangement should be made between local co-ordinating bodies to continue to foster co-operation between local endowed charities. The Expenditure Committee of the House of Commons recommended a sort of roving task force for review but we prefer our own solution.

Co-Ordination of Local Service Charities

186. As we have seen, the precise objective of the review procedure is not specified; there is evidence of different attitudes towards what can and should be achieved, and what the end result should be. Over 16 years even the attitude of the Charity Commission to local reviews has changed. One agreed purpose seems to be to increase the effectiveness of charitable resources where these are:-

(a) held by many small charities in such small amounts as to be ineffective for any purpose unless amalgamation occurs;

(b) held by charities where objects are so outdated that the charity would be ineffective unless the terms of its trust deed could be changed; and

(c) held by a charity which has ceased to be active or where the trustees are unaware of modern needs and thus cannot effectively apply the income.

That local charities should be examined with a view to increases in effectiveness is a good and necessary objective. However, this is easier in the case of endowed trusts, whose purpose is to distribute income from endowments than in the case of charities which provide services other than making grants. In the case of charities which provide a service, a review is much less straightforward, and therefore we would like to comment briefly on the co-ordination and review of local 'service' charities.

As we have mentioned, to our knowledge, no comprehensive review including non-endowed or service charities has been conducted under the provisions of the Charities Act 1960. The charitable 'resources' of these charities would include: income from recurrent voluntary contributions (such as donations, covenants, subscriptions and so forth), from investments, grants from other trusts, grants and payments from local authorities; property owned by the charity such as offices, equipment; facilities connected with its work for the charity, either in paid or unpaid voluntary capacity, whether working at the grass roots or assisting in the administration of the charity. It is obviously important that these resources are used effectively, and managed responsibly. It is equally important that the charity is carrying out valid work, in that it is not simply duplicating what is being done by some other body and that its activity is fulfilling some proven need. However, in seeking to increase effectiveness of local charities, two factors have to be borne in mind:-

(a) charities, whether local or national, are characterised by their methods and distinct approach. This may account for the existence of several charities with similar objects, yet different methods. Thus, duplication can only be proved to exist after the closest examination taking many criteria into account; and

(b) the establishment and continuance of a 'service' charity is usually the response of an individual or group of people wishing to take action for some beneficial social purpose, which is considered charitable in law. It can never be said that a charity exists as some impersonal institution, which just happens to be there, but like any association of human beings there is some deeply personal individual or collective motive. In the case of a service charity, the founder may have been long gone, but the fact that it has to be active to exist, unlike the endowed trust, means that this personal aspect is still very much central to its operation.

This has implications for the review and co-ordination of these charities. The co-operation which exists between local service charities happens on a voluntary basis. Indeed, it could be of harm to both motivation and methods of the charity to co-ordinate activity simply in the name of administrative tidiness, and this is likely to create a hostile and suspicious atmosphere between the charities themselves and the charities and the body which is forcing co-ordination. However, co-operation is of great value and it is desirable to create the very best conditions to foster meaningful co-operation.

At present co-operation exists between service charities locally in a number of ways including:

(a) informal contact between staff, voluntary workers and trustees of local charities;

(b) membership of general umbrella bodies such as a Council for Voluntary Service or a Community Council.

(c) contact through membership of specialised umbrella bodies including organisations working in fields such as youth, the aged, sport, disabled, recreation, women's organisations, and many others;

(d) formal contact through membership of statutory committees, or cross-representation on governing bodies.

We are of the unanimous view that voluntary co-operation between service-providing charities and associated voluntary organisations and between endowed trusts and between these and local government is a most valuable and necessary condition. We are also of the view that the support and encouragement of means by which co-operation can be increased is essential. In many areas throughout the country, support is given by local authorities to bodies such as Councils for Voluntary Service and Community Councils, as well as umbrella bodies for specific groups such as youth organisations, the aged and so forth. This should be encouraged as an effective way of increasing co-operation. However, we would add that strength and co-operation in the voluntary sector depends on local organisations participating to the utmost in the affairs of these bodies, and the quality of co-operation will reflect the level of involvement.

We Recommend

187. **(a) that the review process should be proceeded with as speedily as possible and that the responsibility should be taken from the local authorities and given to the Charity Commission, which should carry it out in liaison with local authorities and local voluntary organisations, such as Community Councils and Councils for Voluntary Service.**

(b) that the reviews should cover all charities, and not be confined to charities for the poor and sick poor.

(c) that wherever practicable Neighbourhood Trusts, or the like, should be set up covering not too large an area in order to retain the local character of the trust.

(d) that powers should be given for trustees of any local trust whose capital assets and income have not exceeded a certain figure on an average over say three years to transfer the trust funds to the Neighbourhood Trust to be held for the purposes of the Neighbourhood Trust irrespective of the terms of the original trust, without the formality of a scheme or *cy-pres* **order.**

(e) that the terms of the Neighbourhood Trusts should be wide covering all the heads of charity, with a special reference to the needs of the locality concerned.

(f) that the review officers should draw the attention of trustees to the benefits of a Neighbourhood Trust.

(g) that, when the review procedure has been completed, arrangements should be made for a permanent local committee to be established under the chairmanship of a representative of the Charity Commissioners to ensure that the process of co-ordination of endowed charities and their co-operation with the welfare services continues after the review. For this purpose full use should be made of existing co-ordinating bodies.

(h) that accounts should be rendered to the local committee and representative of the Charity Commissioners rather than to parish councils.

(i) that in the case of small local endowed charities a power to expend capital should be given subject to appropriate consent by the local committee.

We reject any proposals for compulsory powers of 'municipalisation' as

suggested in the Report of the Expenditure Committee of the House of Commons.

We strongly recommend that assistance should continue to be given to encourage and support co-operation between local service charities; to this end the existing machinery for such co-operation should be supported by local authorities and voluntary bodies as a means of strengthening voluntary co-operation

Part III – Cy-pres Doctrine

Present Powers

188. The Charities Act 1960 does give the Charity Commissioners certain powers to make *cy-pres* schemes other than on the application of the trustees but it does not appear that these powers have ever been used. In particular the Charity Commissioners say that no case has arisen in which the Commissioners have found it necessary to exercise powers under Section 18(6) nor has the Attorney-General ever made an application under Section 18(5). Section 18(6) of the Charities Act 1960 relates to the powers of the Commissioners to apply for authority to make a scheme, when they believe that the trustees by not making an application themselves are acting against the interest of the charity, and, subject to certain conditions, Section 18(5) gives power to the Charity Commissioners to exercise jurisdiction over charities with annual incomes from property of less than £50 on the application made by two or more inhabitants of an area of a charity. This power is sometimes called in aid where the appointments of trustees have either lapsed or have been irregularly made, but it has not been operated in any case on the ground that the trustees themselves were recalcitrant. The Charity Commissioners suggested that it might be useful if the income limitation of £50 a year in Section 18(5) were lifted, as it sometimes happens that the establishment of a scheme is necessary in cases where the income is more than £50 a year and there are no trustess willing to make the application.

Case for Change

189. Doubts have been expressed whether the *cy-pres* rule, is yet sufficiently wide to enable schemes to be made for the best use of charity funds. The Commissioners point out that, while section 13 of the Act of 1960 widened the circumstances in which a *cy-pres* scheme can be made, the provisions of the section are still fairly specific and cannot be ignored in a spirit of robustness. The notion of *cy-pres* implies that the objects of the charity will only be altered to the minimum degree necessary to enable the charity to serve a useful purpose and that otherwise the objects must be kept as near as possible to the objects laid down in the original trust. The question is then whether the *cy-pres* rule should be extended to enable cy-not-so-pres schemes to be made by the Commissioners or the Court, so that the funds might be used for objects satisfying existing local needs, which might well be of a quite different nature to the original trusts, e.g., under some other heading of

charity than that prescribed by the founder. It is, of course, impossible to speculate what the original founder would have thought had he lived at the present time, but the Charity Commissioners told us that, where a Charity for the relief of poverty receives a windfall, as for example, following a profitable sale of land, the Commissioners frequently include provisions in a *cy-pres* scheme enabling the trustees to use the income for other charitable purposes after the need to relieve poverty has been satisfied and they had given trustees a free hand as regards the methods of relieving poverty where these are restricted by the trust deed. They usually include a note at the end of a scheme making suggestions as to how the trustees can make effective use of the funds within the wide discretion given to them. It does mean, therefore, that, in appropriate cases, the Charity Commissioners do not construe the '*cy-pres*' rule very restrictively but it might be useful to clarify the position in any new Act.

190. The procedure for making a scheme is rather complicated in relation to small charities. In a leaflet issued for review organisers by the Charity Commission in May 1968 on the subject of scheme-making, the Commissioners pointed out that, on the making of a scheme, the trusts of the charity have to be assessed to ascertain whether the new proposals are indeed *cy-pres* and whether they are not already wide enough to allow better use of the funds. The area of benefit has to be checked particularly where parish boundaries have been changed since the founding of the charity. The scheme has to be carefully drafted with a certain amount of legal precision. It has to be established that the persons who have applied for the scheme are the proper trustees and that the proper formalities of resolving to apply for the scheme have been complied with. The intention to make a scheme has to be advertised in accordance with the provisions of the Act. It does appear to us that most of these formalities could be dispensed with in a case where the funds of a charity are small especially if the scheme provides for them to be transferred to a Neighbourhood Trust.

191. We think that there are cases where it would be desirable that the objects of a trust should be changed fairly fundamentally and that the Charity Commissioners should have power to order accordingly in appropriate cases. This does not mean that they should always do so and there will continue no doubt to be differences of opinion as to whether the area of operation of a charity should be enlarged or its objects modified while retaining the area. It would be for the Charity Commissioners to decide each case on its merits after hearing the views of the trustees and, in appropriate cases, any representations from local inhabitants.

We Recommend

192. **(a) that the £50 limitation in section 18(5) of the Charities Act 1960 should be removed or at least substantially increased.**

(b) that the formalities of scheme-making be relaxed in relation to

small local charities, especially if the funds of these charities are transferred to Neighbourhood Trusts.

(c) that the *cy-pres* doctrine should be amended or clarified to make it clear that, in appropriate cases a fundamental change in the objects of the charity can be authorised.

Part IV – Review and Co-Ordination of National Charities

Present Powers

193. A good deal of effort is expended on the review of some groups of local charities under the provisions of the Charities Act 1960, and also in fostering co-operation amongst local service charities. However, there are no powers to ensure the review of groups of national charities, although some machinery does exist to foster co-operation amongst some groups and types of national charity. Such co-operation is left to the good sense of trustees, staff and voluntary workers, and, as can be expected, it operates well in certain fields and less well in others.

What is a National Charity?

194. Just as local charities are highly diverse in size, purpose and activities, so too are national charities. The term 'national' is a generic term. It includes charities of all sizes but distinguishes itself from 'local' charities in that its purposes are nationally focused, either in the sense of having a network of branches nationwide (or at least in a majority of counties) or in the sense that they focus their attention on some national government policy. Even as national organisations vary in size so too they are constituted according to no set pattern but can range from Royal Charter to a simple trust instrument.

The Case for Co-Operation

195. In considering the subject of national co-operation there was one overriding argument in our discussions. Charities enjoy many privileges, not least the fiscal and rate reliefs, in return for the benefit they bring to the community. These privileges seem to us to carry responsibilities, one of which is that they seek to co-operate with one another when this is advantageous and when to do otherwise would fail to deploy charitable resources effectively. It is very difficult to draw the perfect balance between a pluralistic approach and a desire to increase efficient administration. We have commented earlier (para. 186) on certain features of service charities which complicate the issue of duplication and effectiveness, which we think are equally relevant to national charities as they are to local. Nevertheless, we would stress the need for co-operation rather than co-ordination. The advantages of co-operation between charities are many: overlap between their fields of work can be decreased, knowledge and information pooled and exchanged; joint action taken on matters of mutual interest; overhead costs such as headquarters, administration and so forth can be reduced; and generally work can become more effective. Some of the

resistance which exists can often come from the collecting charities which are, in a sense, 'competing' for donors, and which feel that collusion or too close co-operation merely means a takeover or dominance by the largest organisation. We know from our enquiries that there are obviously gaps in co-operation, and the Committee heard of examples of lack of co-operation. However, it must be pointed out that, on investigation, the cases which seemed to be outstandingly obvious very often turned out to have quite valid reasons for what appeared to be lack of co-operation.

Present Forms of Co-Operation in the UK

196. The existing formal and informal arrangements for co-operation between various groups of national charities are not unlike the arrangements outlined in para. 186, which relate to local charities. These include:-

(a) informal contact between trustees, staff and voluntary workers of the charity, conferences and seminars on specific areas of policy such as care of the mentally handicapped, youth employment and so forth.

The committee were informed of two such regular 'social' gatherings. One concerns the Chief Executives of some 17 of the major foundations, who have met periodically for about 12 years. Meetings have been on the informal basis but they lead to personal knowledge of one another. More recently, under the pressure of events, the meetings have been directed towards matters of common interest. Discussion on how best to allocate the funds available has never taken place. However, they can with value share information and experience. A case could obviously be put forward for a more formal structure, although voluntary co-operation is preferable to the dangers of forcing co-ordination. Another example is of regular meetings between the general secretaries of charities in the field of handicap where a guest speaker is invited. In addition, there are also examples of regular meetings of specialist staff, such as staff working for the fund-raising and public relations side of national charities, and ad hoc gatherings of charity administrators.

(b) Membership of national associations, federations, standing conferences and councils. Examples of these types of body would include organisations such as the National Old People's Welfare Council, Age Concern, the Central Council for the Disabled, National Council of Voluntary Child Care Organisations. There are also standing conferences covering such fields as drug abuse, youth services and recreational and educational activities of all sorts. The Committee also heard that medical research charities have a standing conference and regular meetings have led to lasting associations and joint activities: for example, joint examination of topics by two organisations that approach the support of research on a disease from different standpoints. It is clear that there is a need for close and regular association between charities and government departments and associated bodies in the same field. However, if charities are to maintain an independent role, they must be free from government 'interference'.

(c) Co-operation can also occur through membership of general umbrella bodies such as the National Council of Social Service. The main types of organisation associated with the NCSS are standing conferences of federations of local organisations and national organisations. Amongst its activities are regular meetings of sub-groups comprising charities and associated voluntary organisations of various interest groups to discuss and exchange information on matters of mutual concern. The success of this machinery for co-operation, in this and other fields, will obviously depend on the degree of involvement and support from its membership, and the value which individual organisations place on co-operation and the advantages it brings. It is interesting to note that similar organisations to the NCSS have been established in many parts of the world, and representatives have the opportunity to meet and exchange ideas through international gatherings such as the International Council on Social Welfare.

(d) Another important aspect of co-operation is the occurrence of frequent ad hoc meetings on matters of particular concern. Examples have included regular meetings on subjects such as: cash and services for the disabled; implementation of the Finer Report on one-parent families: the problem of low income families who cannot pay for their fuel bills; poverty; even we are an example of this - Charity Law.

(e) Representatives of organisations in the various fields will often meet regularly because of their membership of various national voluntary or statutory committees and working groups. Sometimes there is cross-representation on governing bodies.

(f) Finally, it must also be added that a great deal of contact and exchange exists amongst voluntary groups as a result of the publication and dissemination of reports, research findings, articles, newsletters and the like. Some organisations and government departments even produce digests of regular current information which can be received or consulted on request. A brief look at the references in almost any contemporary publication on a topic in the social welfare field will reveal numerous references to publications or internal reports of voluntary organisations.

International Examples

197. With their flair for organisation the Germans have evolved an elaborate system of administration of charities. There is a 'German Foundation Centre' (Stiftungs-zentrum) which concerns itself mainly with endowed foundations and similar bodies. It offers a service which includes data on foundations, literature about them, information, consultation on law and policy, public relations and research. Lest one should think that it is a formidable organisation it should be pointed out that its staff consists of two professionals (one part-time) and two secretaries (one part-time). The Centre is an 'in-house' activity of a

larger body, the Donors' Association for the Promotion of Sciences and Humanities (Stifterverband für die Deutsche Wissenschaft), which is basically a collecting charity and grant-making body and an 'expression of corporate philanthropy'. There may be some lessons to be learnt here, although we are conscious of the severe limitations in making comparisons with other countries due to differences in law, development and even philosophy towards voluntary bodies. As we have said earlier in paras. 186 and 196 (sub-para. c), there are also many other examples of other umbrella bodies which have been set up nationally and locally in other countries, based on the machinery which has developed within the UK.

198. It is not easy to suggest what is the best way to achieve co-operation between charities, and whether there is any need for legislation in respect of this. However, we are of the unanimous view that voluntary co-operation is valuable, and that the law should be used to increase co-operation only in the most extreme cases, and then only in individual cases, such as where objects are outdated, a charity inactive, or the type of duplication remains unjustified, even after the factors which we have outlined earlier have been taken into account. We are of the view that this would be needed very seldom, that the Charity Commissioners already have powers to do this under the existing law, and that even in the few cases which arise, persuasion is better than force. We are also of the view that the existing machinery for voluntary co-operation should be strengthened and encouraged. However, we would make two points on this. Firstly, that if any supervision of charities is sought, it is essential that just as local charities are reviewed, so national charities should be the subject of some review. It is not possible for the voluntary sector to be viewed in a comprehensive fashion, or for government to integrate it into its various policies if little is known about many of the large number of national charities. We would therefore suggest that the Charity Commissioners should initiate a pilot review of national charities in co-operation and consultation with the many umbrella bodies and federations and so forth. Secondly, if the Charity Commission is to fulfil its functions in relation to national charities better than it does at present, it is important that opportunity is given for views of national charities and information about them and their development to be fed into the Commission. For this reason we would suggest that the new Charities Board, which we later recommend, should assist the Charity Commissioners to formulate and constantly update its policy towards national voluntary organisations. The Charity Commissioners told us in evidence that they do not have the necessary expertise, or have on their staff, people with experience of working in the charitable field, to do a great deal more in relation to national charities and associated voluntary organisations at present.

National Charities and Central Government

199. Charities and voluntary organisations at national level will often have formal and informal contacts with various government

departments in the course of their work. At central government level there is a division of responsibility for grant-aiding certain voluntary organisations, and each department deals with the voluntary organisations which come within its field of work. In practice, most of the voluntary bodies funded are registered charities. Since 1973 there has been a development in central government with a view to better co-ordination of government support for voluntary organisations. The Home Office Voluntary Services Unit has been set up with a small annual budget. The object is to 'make grants to voluntary organisations or projects where the work spans the interests of more than one government department (where no other department is able to take the lead) or where no single department has a responsibility'. In general, the Unit's grants go to national organisations but it occasionally provides finance for local projects which have a wider national significance. The VSU takes a close interest in the extent of co-operation between bodies when considering applications for funding, and the extent to which work relates to the areas of greatest social need in both a geographical and a functional sense. The VSU has liaison officers in the main government departments. Special joint seminars are organised from time to time. However, the VSU only have contact with 200 or 300 of the many thousands of charities in existence throughout the country.

Conclusions

200. We are aware that, as with the case of local charities, there is little laid down in law regarding the overall review and co-ordination of national charities. That which exists relates to matters such as scheme-making, *cy-pres*, and other points which relate to individual cases. Therefore a number of the comments that we have made relate to the general functions of the Charity Commissioners and policies which we feel they should adopt. We have a feeling that there is still a great deal to be gained in encouraging co-operation between national charities, and that the policy of government and the Charity Commissioners should openly encourage the further development of means of co-operation as outlined earlier. A good deal of further encouragement could be given to charities to share services, where this is possible, and advice can be given to new charities or to charities whose activities are examined during the review period that we suggested in an earlier chapter (para. 142) to this end. However, we have concluded that this should be achieved, except in the most extreme cases, by persuasion rather than force.

We Recommend

201. (a) **that co-operation between national charities should be developed and encouraged by persuasion, and not by legal means, and that full advantage should be taken of the existing umbrella bodies, federations and so forth to achieve this. To this end such bodies should be given support and encouragement by government and the Charity Commissioners;**

(b) **that the Charity Commissioners should initiate a review in the**

form of a survey or series of surveys to determine to what extent greater effectiveness could be achieved by further co-operation; and that this should be done with the assistance of existing umbrella bodies and federations; and

(c) the new Charities Board which we recommend later should assist the Charity Commission in the formulation of policy towards national charities and their development, and bring outside experience of charities into the Charity Commission.

Part V – Statutory Controls on Fund Raising

The Legislation

202. We thought it necessary to examine the controls on fund raising and to see whether existing controls are adequate or should be strengthened, or on the other hand relaxed. There are three main Acts controlling fund raising by charities. They are the War Charities Act 1940, which is applied to charities for disabled persons by the National Assistance Act 1948; the House to House Collections Act 1939 and the Police, Factories, etc, (Miscellaneous Provisions) Act 1916, Section 5 of which governs street collections. These Acts seem to have been passed in a rather piecemeal fashion no doubt as a result of specific scandals which hit the headlines at the time. There is no general statute which prevents appeals to the public by charities. War charities and charities for disabled persons cannot make any appeal to the public unless they are registered. Other charities are only controlled as regards house-to-house collections and street collections. There are different provisions as to registration, exemptions, appeals, and grounds for refusal of registration under each of these Acts.

War Charities and Charities for the Disabled

203. 'War Charities' mean 'charities having for their sole or principal object the relief of distress caused or the supply of needs or comfort to persons affected by the two World Wars or any war or act of aggression to which the Act is declared to be applicable'. The Charity Commissioners can determine whether a charity is a war charity. War Charities cannot appeal to the public for donations or raise money by bazaars, entertainments, etc., unless registered under the 1940 Act. The registration authorities are London borough councils, councils for non-metropolitan counties and metropolitan districts, the Common Council of the City of London and the Council of the Isles of Scilly. Exemption can be granted by the registration authority on the ground that the charity being established in good faith is of a limited character. Registration must be refused unless there is a management committee of at least three people and may be refused if the charity is not established or is not being carried on in good faith; is not being or likely to be properly administered; if the total money likely to be applied towards the objects is inadequate in proportion to the total collected; if remuneration is excessive or if the authority does not get sufficient information on the above points. There is an appeal to the Charity

Commissioners. The registration authority can require accounts as frequently as they think necessary. A charity can be removed from the register by a registration authority which must do so if directed by the Charity Commissioners after investigation. It seems to us that some 30 years since the last World War that Parliament might look at the provisions for the control and regulation of war charities with a view to repealing them. The War Charities Act and regulations made under it are applied to charities for "disabled persons". The phrase refers to charities having for their sole or for their sole or principal object the promotion of the welfare of the blind, deaf or dumb or other persons substantially or permanently handicapped by disability. There is an additional ground for refusing to register a charity for disabled persons and that is if their objects are adequately attained by a registered charity. Originally the control applied to collections for the blind. We think that these regulations for the control of charities for disabled persons should continue but a new Act should be introduced for this purpose.

House-to-House Collections

204. The House to House Collections Act 1939 applies to collections for any charitable, benevolent or philanthropic purpose, whether charitable or not. The promoter, unless exempt, must get a licence, the licensing authority being in this case the Common Council of the City of London, the Commissioner of Appeals in the Metropolitan Police District and elsewhere the District Council of the locality. Exemption can be granted either locally or by a chief officer of police if the collection is local in character and of short duration or nationally by the Secretary of State if the area of the charity covers the whole or a substantial part of England. The grounds on which a licensing authority may refuse or revoke the grant of a licence are that the total likely to be applied for the purposes of the charity is inadequate in proportion to takings; that excessive remuneration is likely to be retained; that the grant of the licence would facilitate begging; that the applicant is not a fit and proper person to hold a licence by reason of conviction for certain offences; that the applicant has failed to exercise due diligence in choice of collectors and in seeing that they obey the rules; or that he has not given sufficient information. There is an appeal this time to the Secretary of State who also makes regulations prescribing the form of certificate of authority, badges, receipt books and other matters relating to the collection. Under these regulations no person under 16 years can collect, no one must importune or remain at the door of a house if asked to leave, the donor must put the money straight into a collecting box or have a receipt, except that envelope collections can be authorised if the charitable purpose is of major importance and the collection is suitably administered. Accounts of the collection must be sent to the licensing authority within one month of the expiry of the licence or annually to the Secretary of State in case of charities exempted by him.

205 Contrary to what seems to have been common belief, local authorities have no power to refuse a licence on the grounds that

proposed collecting dates clash with those of another collection already planned, nor have they authority to limit collecting dates. They grant a licence for the period specified in the application which must not exceed 12 months. The Joint Select Committee, on whose recommendations the 1939 Act was passed, specifically recommended against the licensing authorities being given powers to limit collections on the view, which Parliament endorsed, that the freedom of individuals and organisations to promote house-to-house collections should be restricted to the extent necessary to ensure that they are bona fide and the collection properly conducted. In practice, however, local authorities have tended to try to restrict the number of collections in their areas and to adopt this policy in relation to charities which are not exempted. The Secretary of State informs licensing authorities of exemptions and, as a result of a conference organised by the NCSS in 1973, proposals were made for a voluntary system of local registers of collecting dates and it was emphasised that the exempt charities should notify licensing authorities of their proposed dates.

Street Collections

206. Regulations as to street collections are made by police authorities and may differ from district to district. The only ones published as a statutory instrument are those made for the Metropolitan Police District other than the City of London. A permit has to be obtained from the Commissioner of Police and applications must be made in the name of a committee or other body consisting of not less than three persons. The permit will mention the day, time and areas where the collection can take place. Collectors must not obstruct or annoy anyone. They must occupy a stationary position, not more than two at one place, must not be under 16 years of age, they cannot use a table so as to cause obstructions or any table exceeding 30 inches in length and 20 inches in width. They must not use a box at the end of a pole to reach upper windows or roofs of conveyances. They must present a box numbered and securely closed and bearing permanently the name of the fund. They must not be paid for their services. Accounts must be rendered within a month to the Commissioner.

Views of Local Authorities

207. We discussed the statutory controls with representatives of the Association of District Councils. They had no comments on war charities and charities for the disabled which are the responsibilty of the county councils. They did not feel that similar provisions should apply to all charities making appeals to the public other than by house-to-house or street collections. They felt that there was no point in imposing new administrative controls of this sort upon local charities in general unless real need was proved. The representatives of the metropolitan authorities thought that no particular difficulties arose in the operation of this legislation. Most of the charities which appealed to the public were known to them and any phoney charities fairly quickly got reported and appropriate action would be taken by the police.

There is some doubt whether war charities present any problem meriting special control at the present time.

208. The House to House Collections Act was the subject of a good deal of interest among district councils. They did not think that the system whereby, on the one hand, the police could exempt small temporary charities, and, on the other, the Home Office could exempt the larger charities was satisfactory and they thought that the licensing of house-to-house collections should be left entirely with the local authority and both these forms of exemption taken away. They felt that the Home Office exemption resulted in overlapping between the large charities and the small local ones, often with disastrous effects to the latter. There was no statutory requirement that the exempt charity should notify local authorities of the dates on which they intended to carry out house-to-house collections. The voluntary arrangements made for exempt charities to inform district councils of the proposed dates of their collections did not appear always to work well and the district councils felt that there should be a requirement of 12 months' notice by exempt charities of their proposed dates of collection. These suggestions seem to postulate that the licensing authorities do have power to regulate the dates of collection by non-exempt charities.

Views of Certain Charities

209. Naturally the point of view of the exempt charities, of which there are 58, is different. They plan their campaigns on a national basis and to have to negotiate separately with 371 district councils would impose considerable hardship upon them. The general policy of the Home Office since the transfer of licensing to the district councils has been to grant exemptions to charities collecting in 70 or more areas. This difficulty particularly confronts charities which do not have an immediate popular appeal, however useful the purpose they be serving. Whereas there is always an immediate response to appeals for cancer research there is less response in the case of epilepsy or mental diseases. The less popular charities may find it difficult to obtain a supply of voluntary workers and may therefore be compelled to employ paid collectors who move from area to area. The British Epilepsy Association gave us strong evidence to this effect. They told us that if they lost their exemption certificate they would have to register with at least 30 local authorities and to the considerable detriment of their own organisational effectiveness. Possession of an exemption certificate means that they are not limited as to the length of time that their collectors operate in a particular local authority area. If they apply to a local authority they would be given permission to collect during one week only and they certainly would not be able, with their resources, to realise the full financial potential of that area. As it is, they find it difficult to maintain collections on a scale sufficient to justify their exemption. In fact during the course of this inquiry the exemption granted to the British Epilepsy Association has been withdrawn by the Home Office.

210. Representatives of the district councils pointed out, with some justice, that the exemption system does not apply to street collections and the national charities do not seem to find this a handicap. Street collections, as already mentioned, are licensed by the police authorities, that is, the police committee of the county councils. Usually the larger charities manage to tie them in with their house-to-house collections.

211. Two minor points arose during the discussions:-

(a) A recent case decided that a public house was a house for the purpose of the House to House Collections Act but that to prove an offence under the Act it was necessary to show that the collector had gone from house to house and therefore if a collection was made in a single public house it was not a house-to-house collection. The representatives of the district councils felt that there was a good deal of opportunity for abuse in public house collections, particularly around Christmas, and that anyone making such a collection should have to register and account to the local authority, which seems to us a sensible proposal.

(b) It has been suggested to us in evidence that the age limit for collectors in respect of house-to-house collections and street collections should be reduced to 15, releasing perhaps a further supply of voluntary workers. The representatives of the local authority felt that there was no harm in 15-year-olds taking part in street collections but that it might be undesirable for them to go from house to house in certain areas and we are inclined to agree with this view.

Conclusions

212. The opposing points of view on the main argument are very difficult to reconcile, but the licensing authorities' point of view only seems to us to make sense on the basis that they do have power to specify the dates on which non-exempt bodies can carry out house-to-house collections in their area. Equally, if exemption is only against satisfying each district council of the suitability of the charity to run house-to-house collections, there seems no point in further restrictions on exempt charities, since if the charity is a national one the vetting could best be done by the Home Secretary, to whom any local complaints about their collectors could be forwarded by the local authority. The real question is whether the law should be strengthened to enable district councils to control the collecting dates of non-exempt charities. Only on this basis is there a case for abolishing or restricting exemptions. We understand that the problem of house-to-house collections varies enormously from one locality to another. In some there are probably an excessive number of house-to-house collections; in others hardly any at all. We feel that the system needs to be revised. We have sympathy with the view that in areas where there is a real problem the number of house-to-house collections should be restricted and the local charities should be given a fair crack of the whip. The vetting functions in relation to larger national charities should

continue to be exercised by the Secretary of State but they should be encouraged to extend their activities into areas which at present do not experience many collections. The present voluntary system does not seem to work everwhere satisfactorily and perhaps a solution would be to allow district councils in areas where there are too many collections to be authorised by the Secretary of State to allocate collecting dates in those particular areas, giving due consideration to those national charities which, by their nature, collect nation-wide during a particular week.

We Recommend

213. **(a) That Parliament might consider repealing the provisions relating to war charities but that charities for the disabled should remain as they are and new legislation introduced to regulate and control them.**

(b) that the procedures relating to the licensing of house-to-house collections should be revised to enable local authorities, with the consent of the Secretary of State, to co-ordinate collecting dates in those areas where the number of charities operating house-to-house collections is excessive; in other areas exempt charities should give reasonable notice of their dates of house-to-house collection to local authorities so as to enable the voluntary system to be operated more efficiently.[1]

(c) that a person making a collection for a charity in a public house should have the same obligation to register and account to the district council as persons collecting from house to house.

(d) that the regulations as to street collections should be modified to permit collection by persons of 15 years of age.

Part VI – Other Controls On Fund Raising

The Present Position

214. Apart from the statutory controls, there is no limitation on methods of fund raising other than the ordinary criminal law. For instance, it is open to anyone to make an appeal to the public for funds for a charitable or indeed non-charitable object through advertisements in the media (subject to the voluntary controls on advertisements exercised by the bodies concerned) or by circulars sent through the post. Appeals for charitable objects can be made not only by bodies which are registered charities but by any other body or individual and two cases were publicised in the press during the course of our inquiries which illustrate this point. In one, a man was

[1] One member of the Committee dissents from this recommendation and would prefer to see house-to-house collections brought under the same control as street collections. (This would avoid the annoyance to the public caused by a house-to-house collection being held by more than one charity in the same area in the same week and would avoid the 'competition' which at present can (and does) arise between a local charity and a national charity which holds a Home Office Exemption Certificate but may not undertake any local activities in the area.)

prosecuted for embezzling funds of what was believed to be a charity but was acquitted because the accounts were in a chaotic state. The judge ordered the Charity Commissioners to investigate the position and it was found that the body from which he was alleged to have embezzled the money was not itself a charity, although it was closely connected with a charity with a similar name. In another, 'The Times' newspaper, after protests from an established charity, cancelled an advertisement for medical research inserted in the personal columns by a man on behalf of a company which was not a charity. It is obvious that no examination of the accounts of charities by the Charity Commissioners could have revealed these situations. Further there is nothing which prescribes the percentage of monies received which has to be used for research or handed over to a charity by the collector in such cases.

Is Control Necessary?

215. We have given a great deal of thought to the question whether there should be some pre-condition to be satisfied before any individual or organisation makes appeals to the public for money for purposes which might be charitable or analogous to charitable purposes. In particular, should any of the statutory provisions above referred to be extended to charities other than war charities and charities for the disabled and to methods of collecting funds other than house-to-house collections and street collections? We asked the Charity Commissioners whether there was any logic behind the special treatment of war charities and charities for the disabled and they thought that the reason was that these were the types of charity which were most likely to be used by confidence tricksters. Certainly very little evidence has come to our notice of abuses or dishonesty in relation to charities and such abuses by way of bogus charities as may exist are more a matter for the police than for surveillance by the Charity Commissioners. We have already, however, recommended (para. 141) that new charities on registration should file with the Charity Commission details of the sources of their assets and revenue. This suggestion might be extended to make it compulsory for all charities which intend to make appeals of any sort to the public to file some sort of statement as to the methods which they intend to use and to supplement this from time to time with further statements, if and when they are proposing to change their methods and adopt new methods. It might then be an offence to make an appeal to the public except in accordance with the filed statement. It is not thought that anything in the nature of a prospectus as required by the Companies Acts in relation to appeals to the public for subscription to shares would be appropriate to charities for whom fund raising is a continuous process, but a simple statement of the sort mentioned might be appropriate.

There remains the question of collections for charities by outside individuals or bodies or collections by such bodies or individuals for purposes which could be regarded as charitable. That some control is desirable seems obvious, but it is difficult to draw the line. For instance, a number of school children may go on a sponsored walk with a view to handing the proceeds to a charity. Other people collect milk bottle tops or silver paper or old newspapers and postage stamps and raise money for charities in this way. On the other hand without some control there is a danger that, without any breach of the ordinary laws of the land, there may be serious abuses.

Conclusions

216. This is a sensitive subject. At first sight there seems little logic in confining the vetting procedure to war charities and charities for the disabled and a strong argument for saying that, before any appeal is made to the public, there should be something in the nature of a prospectus, however rudimentary. As regards registered charities, we feel that this can be covered by –

(a) the requirement we have suggested that a statement should be filed on registration stating how the charity proposes to achieve its objects;

(b) the requirement mentioned later that a report should be filed with the accounts;

(c) the procedure already suggested for reviewing registered charities which have been provisionally registered; and

(d) the provisions which we have already suggested for local surveillance of local charities.

As regards other appeals, it would seem reasonable to require some control and the best form of control would appear to us to be a licensing procedure similar to that under the House to House Collections Act before any appeal is sent to the public through the post or through the media for an object of a charitable nature or one which would be taken by the public to be charitable.

We Recommend

217. **(a) that apart from the measures mentioned in the previous paragraph, no further controls on appeals to the public should be imposed on registered charities.**

(b) that no one other than a person authorised by a registered charity should be permitted to make an appeal to the public by post or through the media for an object of a charitable nature or one which could be taken by the public to be charitable unless that person registers with and is accountable to the district council in the area where he resides or carries on business in the same way as for a charity under the House to House Collections Act.

Part VII – Other Points on Fund Raising

Code of Practice

218. The methods adopted by collecting charities to raise funds are many and various and new ideas are always being thought up. Some of these methods might be regarded as dubious. The National Council of Social Service considered charitable fund raising in 1968 and set up a

working party which called for evidence of reports of abuse made to the Charity Commissioners. They found that, so far as this evidence was concerned, abuse was minimal and they thought that a code of practice could not be enforced but suggested a voluntary code of practice which could be adopted by charities. Their recommendations which were that the promoters of charitable appeals to the public, whether for money or for gifts in kind, should:-

(1) Make clear the charitable objects for which the appeal is made and whether the proceeds are to be applied direct or given to other agencies for this purpose.

(2) Be satisfied that those objects are reasonably possible of attainment.

(3) Give their name and address.

(4) Define precisely what gifts in kind are required and whether for distribution or sale.

(5) Use only lawful and reputable fund-raising methods.

(6) Do everything possible to ensure that, if expenses are to be incurred in connection with an appeal, a commensurate return over a reasonable period is obtained.

(7) Make sure that if fund-raising methods are adopted which entail the deduction of expenses before any proceeds accrue to the charity, the public are left in no reasonable doubt of the fact. This applies especially if the appeal is made in association with commercial or other non-charitable persons or bodies, or by trading.

(8) Apply the proceeds of the appeal for the objects stated, either by cash grants, by the provision of supplies, by personal services (paid or voluntary) or in such other ways as are conducive to the attainment of the objects of the appeal.

(9) Administer the proceeds efficiently, economically and in a businesslike manner, employing suitable paid staff when necessary.

(10) Produce proper reports and keep proper accounts (the latter being a statutory requirement).

219. Furthermore, the report went on to recommend that, if the promoters of any charitable appeal to the public are appealing on behalf of an existing charity they should:-

(1) First obtain the charity's authority for the appeal.

(2) Conform to its requirements in conducting the appeal.

(3) Give its name and address in the appeal, as well as their own.

(4) Account to the authorising charity for the proceeds of the appeal in such manner as the charity may require.

By giving its authority the charity concerned thereby accepts responsibility for the appeal.

Administration Expense

220. Another problem which causes criticism from time to time is the proportion between administration on the one hand and the amount available for the charitable purpose on the other. This is something which has to be taken into consideration by the registration authorities under the statutory provisions already referred to, but it is impossible to lay down any uniform rule. The differences between fund-raising charities and endowed trusts, between those who collect money and pass it on to other charities and those who do charitable work themselves make it impossible to define any limit. Saving on administrative expenses is not always an effective criterion by which to judge the efficient use of charitable resources, as weak administration can often lead to wastage and loss of effectiveness. But the expenses should be clearly and correctly detailed in charity accounts, distinguishing between purely administrative expenses and expenses incidental to the fulfilling of the charity's function.

Consultants

221. The employment of fund-raising consultants is another practice which has been criticised. It is said that they lessen the confidence of the public in the charity and cause suspicion that they are taking too large a percentage for themselves. We have heard evidence on this both from charities and from a representative of a well-known firm of professional fund-raisers. Where it is necessary to raise a large amount of money in a single appeal over a comparatively short period, eg, for the repair of a cathedral or the establishment of a foundation to commemorate a distinguished citizen recently deceased, there is much to be said for the employment of a professional fund-raiser, provided that great care is taken in the choice of a fund-raiser and in the terms of the contract. There are probably not enough concerns in this field to insist on some professional organisation with a code of professional conduct, but we have considered the question whether fund-raising consultants should be required to register with the Charity Commissioners and whether any model form of contract should be drawn up from which the parties could only depart with the consent of the Charity Commissioners.

Lotteries and Football Pools

222. A particular problem concerns lotteries and football pools. As regards the former an Act has recently been passed which partly assists charities and partly is regarded as potentially detrimental by them. The good news is the raising of financial limits in Sections 43 and 45 of the Betting Gaming and Lotteries Act 1963. The bad news is to allow local authorities to promote lotteries which at present they are not permitted to do. The financial limits were last fixed 12 years ago and in present-day terms were unrealistic and this alteration is certainly welcomed. On the other hand, charities are apprehensive that the inclusion of local authorities in this field will diminish their own effectiveness as a method of fund raising. Lotteries have been found to be a useful method of fund raising for charities since the combination of

giving to charity and the chance to win money is attractive to the ordinary man. It is felt that the amount which can be raised by charities locally will be greatly affected by the inclusion of local authorities. Local authorities could have an advantage over charities since they could advertise their lotteries in rate demands and through rent collectors from council tenants, in public libraries, clinics, swimming baths, and even with the help of their dustmen. Time will show whether the apprehension of local charities is justified. Football pools present a different problem. In charity football pools the punter exercises no skill but buys a numbered ticket which is related to the results of certain matches and for this reason charity football pools were declared by the House of Lords to be a lottery and illegal. Some charities, notably the Spastics Society, derive a very large proportion of their income from pools and it is hoped that the Pools Competition Act 1971, which is extended year by year, will be replaced by some permanent Act making charity football pools legal.

Special Sources of Revenue

223. In connection with fund raising, perhaps some mention should be made of the sources sometimes available to the smaller charities in the form of public grants and grants from foundations. We have the impression that many small charities are not aware of these possible sources of assistance. The Voluntary Service Unit of The Home Office assists some charities and voluntary organisations whose function does not fall within the remit of any one government department, and in certain circumstances will co-ordinate its grant-making policy with local authorities and with other public bodies and foundations who also give grant aid according to various criteria. There is also an increasing number of foundations created for general charitable purposes or general charitable purposes in particular fields and it is open to the smaller charities to apply to these foundations for a grant in suitable cases. In the case of charities whose objects have no immediate popular appeal, these sources of funds could be of the greatest importance and we would draw the attention of trustees of such charities to the existence of these possible solutions to some of their problems.

We Recommend

224. **(a) that trustees of charities should be made aware of the NCSS proposed voluntary code and that non-compliance with it should be taken into account on any review of charities.**

(b) that consultants undertaking fund raising for reward should register with the Charity Commissioners, who should have a model form of contract which should apply in all cases unless the Charity Commissioners otherwise consent.

(c) that local authorities in deciding whether or not to run lotteries should bear in mind the possible loss to local charities.

(d) that charity football pools should be permanently legalised.

Part VIII – Accountability of Charities

Statutory Provisions

225. The statutory provisions relating to accounts are as follows:-

(a) Charity trustees must keep proper books of accounts and unless their accounting is prescribed by an Act other than the Charities Act 1960 they must prepare consecutive statements of account consisting on each occasion of an income and expenditure account relating to a period of not more than 15 months and a balance sheet relating to the end of that period (Charities Act 1960 Sect.32 (1)).

(b) Statements of account relating to a parochial charity in a rural parish other than an ecclesiastical charity are to be sent annually to the parish council or, if there is no parish council, to the chairman of the parish meeting (Sect.32 (3)).

(c) Statements of account are to be transmitted yearly without any request to the Charity Commissioners by charities having a permanent endowment in respect of that permanent endowment, unless the charity is excepted by order or regulations, and on request any charity must send statements of account relating to all its affairs.

(d) All such accounts are open to public inspection so long as they are preserved by the Commissioners (Sect.8(2)).

(e) The Commissioners can order an audit by a professional auditor, the expenses being borne by the Commissioners (Sect.8(3), (4), (5)).

(f) If trustees do not comply, the Commissioners can give such directions as they think appropriate (Sect.8(6)).

(g) Section 8 does not apply to an exempt charity (Sect.8(7)).

(h) If the charity is incorporated under the Companies Acts, then its accounts will have to comply with those Acts. Also those charities which are required to register with other bodies, by virtue of various statutes (e.g., the Friendly Society Acts) have to send their accounts to the Registrar of those bodies as well as to the Charity Commissioners.

Scrutiny by the Charity Commissioners

226. The Charity Commissioners do not claim to be, neither are they constituted to be, auditors of the accounts and for this reason and since they have the statutory power to order an audit by professional auditors they do not have an accountant on their staff. When they examine accounts they scrutinise them to see that expendable funds are being applied for charitable purposes and in accordance with the trusts to see that there is no obvious inefficiency in management either of the charity or its property; that it is not in apparent danger of insolvency; that trusts are still capable of being carried out; and that expendable funds are being used without any excessive accumulation of money in hand. They also check that the income from the investments appears to be adequate and complies with the Trustee Investments Act 1961. They may also check for apparently unduly high administrative expenses, that tax and rate relief is being recovered, and any rentcharge income is being actually received.

227. The Charity Commissioners are not able to examine the accounts of all the registered non-exempt charities each year and for a period they did not carry out any examination at all. They now examine between 6,000 and 7,000 a year out of the 115,000 charities. They concentrate on new charities and try to examine the accounts of most charities about once every five years. The examination of accounts quite frequently is followed by recommendations which may sometimes lead to a scheme being made to bring the charity's objects and administration up to date.

Responsibility of Charities

228. The Committee's discussions have highlighted the need for charities and voluntary bodies to be subjected to disciplines consistent with the size of their assets and their responsibilities. At the highest levels, disciplines as strict as those applicable to a public company under the stringent provisions of the Companies Acts may well be appropriate. At the other end of the scale, for instance, a small parish charity for the poor, a simple set of accounts looked at by a local retired bank manager or someone like that may be the appropriate procedure.

229. The current position so far as charities are concerned is contained in the Charities (Statements of Account) Regulations 1960 (SI 1960 No.2525) which details the minimum information to be included in statements of account and this information, where appropriate, should be applicable to all charities whatever size. The schedule states that the information so provided must include:-

(a) particulars of the assets and the persons in whom they are vested and the date of the year to which the charity's accounts are made up, distinguishing between assets forming part of the permanent endowment and other assets;

(b) the appropriate amount of the liabilities on that day;

(c) the amount of the receipts in the year ending on that day classified according to the nature of the receipt and distinguishing between receipts forming part of the permanent endowment and other assets;

(d) the amount of the payments made during that year classified according to the nature of the payment and distinguishing between payments made out of the permanent endowment and other payments.

Form of Accounts

230. The Charity Commissioners have forms for statements of account. There are two sets, one for use by charities which do not possess land and one for charities which do possess land or interest in land such as rent charges but the Charity Commissioners do not insist on the use of these forms which are somewhat complex in character. That appears to be reasonable.

231. In the case of charities of any significant size, it is essential that all accounts should abide by the following requirements:-

(a) **Expenditure**

(i) Administration costs should be separated from expenditure on the objectives of the charity.

(ii) Expenditure on the objectives of the charity should be further sub-divided between long-term expenditure, i.e., where continuing commitments have been entered into and short-term or one-off type expenditure.

(iii) Administration costs should not include fund-raising costs which should therefore be separately identified and there may be a case for deducting these costs from the actual income received showing both gross and net income on the income side of the accounts.

(b) **Income**

(i) Long-term income received from interest on investments and endowments should be separated from short and medium-term income arising from covenants, etc.

(ii) Occasional income, i.e., donations and the results of fund-raising appeals, should also be separately shown.

(c) **Asset Structure**

The asset structure could usefully be broken down to demonstrate, certainly amongst the larger charities, the assets available in terms of, for example, properties and equipment for long-term serving of the charity's objectives.

Audit

232. Unless the charity is registered under the Companies Acts and subject to their disciplines, there is no statutory requirement for its accounts to be professionally audited. No doubt in many cases a charity will automatically have its accounts audited by professional accountants. Nevertheless we think that there ought to be included in any new legislation a provision for professional auditing of accounts if the income of a charity exceeds a certain figure. The figure would be governed by practicability in relation to fees taking into consideration any offer by the professional bodies to make available services at reduced fees or on a voluntary basis. Charities with smaller incomes should be subject to an independent audit.

Report to Accompany Accounts

233. Another point which has been suggested to us is that there should be filed with the accounts a report of the activities of the charity including its policy and any changes in its methods. Again the Companies Act require a great many matters to be included in the directors' report which accompanies the accounts and some of these may be relevant to particular charities, but we do feel that an appropriate kind of report which states in general language what the charity has been doing during the year is of great importance. There has been a good deal of controversy as to the extent to which charities should publish detailed expenditure accounts of their charitable

purposes. This is a particularly acute problem in relation to grant-giving foundations. Those accounts and reports filed with the Charity Commissioners are open to inspection by the public, but they do not normally give a great deal of information as to what the charity does, and where its objects are listed 'as general charitable purposes' normally very little can be deduced as to its activities. The information has, of course, to be given to the Revenue for tax purposes and it is normally we understand given to the Charity Commissioners, but the practice varies as to the extent to which information is published or given to inquirers. There may be good reasons in many cases why this information should not be made public in too much detail, but unless there are such reasons the greater the publicity the better. A demand for publicity was forcibly raised by one body which gave us evidence. They mentioned a case where a grant-giving charity which had been accustomed to make known to the public details of loans and donations made to and by it changed its practice and refused to give more details than those filed with the Charity Commissioners. This is ideally a point upon which the Charities Board which we recommend in the succeeding paragraphs of this report could give guidance from time to time and it would be open to the Charity Commissioners under existing powers to make regulations defining what information has to be given. At one end of the scale one would not expect a parochial charity to disclose to the world the name of the widow who received assistance. At the other end it may be said that responsible and interested people should be able to satisfy themselves as to the way in which charitable sums, particularly those collected from the public, are being disbursed to be sure that they are used most efficiently.

Conclusions and Recommendations

234. We do not wish to impose undue and unnecessary administrative burdens on charities, particularly the smaller charities, but we do think that all charities should account for their activities at the appropriate level; and that the form of accounts should more clearly comply with the requirements which we have already mentioned. We do not think that the proportion of accounts which are checked annually by the Charity Commissioners is all that adequate. Accordingly,

We Recommend:

(a) that local accounts should be checked by the local committees which we are proposing under the chairmanship of a representative of the Charity Commissioners.

(b) that there should be statutory requirement of professional audit of accounts where the income exceeds a certain figure, for smaller incomes, the audit should be independent.

(c) that the staff of the Charity Commissioners should be sufficient at least to enable the accounts of all new charities to be examined for the first three years of their existence and of all charities to be examined not less frequently than every five years.

(d) That the Charity Commissioners should have sufficient staff with

accountancy skills to advise whether the system of preparing accounts is adequate to give relevant information to the public.

(e) The accounts should be accompanied by a report (perhaps included in the annual report) setting out in sufficient terms the activities of the charity during the year in question and its intentions during the succeeding year.

(f) that the question of how much detailed information should be given to the public about the expenditure of charities on their charitable objects should be reviewed from time to time by the Charity Commissioners with the assistance of the Charities Board which we later recommend and the necessary regulations made from time to time.

Chapter VIII

Structure of the Charity Commission

Criticisms of the Commission

235. The Nathan Committee found that the image of the Charity Commissioners was far from satisfactory and urged them to do something about it. Nearly 25 years later we find much the same criticisms being levelled against the Charity Commissioners as were being levelled at the time of the Nathan Committee. A fine selection of vituperative epithets has been levelled at them in the evidence. We do not think that these criticisms are justified. The Charity Commissioners are in fact circumscribed in their functions by the terms of the Act and in contrast to the criticisms there have also been many witnesses who have spoken of their helpfulness. We have considerable sympathy for them since they have had a difficult task to perform which does not give them much scope for creative work. The fact that they are all permanent civil servants inhibits them in projecting a vigorous image of themselves and their annual reports, though well written, do not make any great impact upon the public.

236. The Nathan Committee recommended that there should be a lay element in the Charity Commission itself and also that they should have the help of an advisory body which should assist them to test proposed policies, but one of the troubles is that there are very few respects under the present set-up in which the Charity Commissioners have any function involving policy-making. Indeed, before considering the structure of the Charity Commission, we have asked ourselves why a charity commission is necessary, what it does at present and what we think it should do.

Present Functions

237. The general function of the Charity Commissioners under the Charities Act 1960 is to promote the effective use of charitable resources by encouraging the development of better methods of administration, by giving charity trustees information or advice on any matter affecting the charity and by investigating and checking abuses. The Act directs that it shall be the general object of the Commissioners, so to act in the case of any charity (unless it is a matter of altering its purposes) as best to promote and make effective the work of the charity in meeting the needs designated by its trusts. But the Commissioners have not themselves power to act in the administration of a charity. The specific powers and duties given to the Commissioners by the Act, in the order in which they appear in the Act include:

(a) to provide charities with the service of an Official Custodian for Charities (who is one of their officers)

(b) to establish and maintain a register of charities in which will be entered every charity not excepted by sub-section (4) of Section 4 of the Charities Act 1960

(c) to decide which organisations and trusts are charitable in law and to remove from the register any institution which no longer appears to the Commissioners to be a charity as well as any charity which ceases to exist or does not operate

(d) to institute inquiries into charities where necessary

(e) to receive accounts of charities

(f) to supply local authorities with copies of such entries in the register of charities as are needed for a local index

(g) to receive reports and recommendations from local authorities as a result of local reviews

(h) to make orders, in exercise of the same jurisdiction as the High Court, for the following purposes:

- (i) to establish schemes for the administration of charities (this includes *cy-pres* schemes);
- (ii) to appoint and remove trustees and officers of charities;
- (iii) to vest or transfer property belonging to a charity (including vesting property in the Official Custodian for Charities)

(j) to frame schemes to be brought into effect by Parliament by means of statutory instrument

(k) to give consent to a charity incurring expenditure in promoting a private bill for Parliament

(l) to protect charity property in cases of misconduct or mismanagement by freezing assets or removing trustees and appointing others

(m) to appoint Trustees of a charity that has no trustees, without needing an application

(n) to establish common investment schemes

(o) to authorise transactions by a charity, thereby giving the trustees power which they might otherwise have lacked

(p) to advise trustees on the performance of their duties, thereby protecting the trustees against a charge of breach of trust

(q) to require the redemption of rent charges belonging to charities

(r) to decide whether or not to authorise a charity to take charity proceedings in court

(s) to decide whether or not to give consent to the sale (and other disposition) of permanent endowment (and other) land belonging to a charity

(t) to report each year to the Secretary of State.

New Functions Proposed

238. The additional tasks which we have suggested should be undertaken by the Charity Commission are the following:-

(a) to keep under review newly created charities and take what steps are necessary in relation to those which are not being efficiently run or are not performing any charitable services which could not be better performed by or in conjunction with another charity (para. 142)

(b) to take action in the case of so-called disaster funds to decide between more than one fund and to provide help in setting them up, maintaining for this purpose appropriate model trust deeds (para. 166)

(c) to take over the responsibility for instituting and supervising local reviews (para. 185)

(d) to provide inspectors or regional officers who will preside over local committees for the surveillance of local charities and for encouraging their co-ordination and co-operation after reviews have been completed (para. 185)

(e) to institute a survey or series of surveys relating to national charities and to take such steps as may seem necessary as a result of such surveys to foster co-operation and greater efficiency (para. 200)

(f) to increase the extent of their study of accounts of charities so that at least they can look at such accounts yearly in the case of new charities and every five years in the case of all other charities (para. 234)

(g) to review from time to time the amount of detailed information made available to the public by charities as to their sources of income and the application of their funds (para. 233)

(h) to provide appropriate secretarial and administrative assistance to the Charities Board, which is described later (para. 243)

(i) to consult the Charities Board on certain matters, as described later (para. 244).

Lay Element

239. We think that the new tasks which we are suggesting that the Charity Commissioners should undertake do involve more in the way of value judgements than their present functions, which are largely semi-judicial or purely administrative. These considerations have revived the argument that a lay element should be introduced in the governing body and that there should be created an independent advisory body, as suggested by the Nathan Committee.

240. We doubt however whether the introduction of a lay element into the Charity Commission itself would work satisfactorily The great bulk of the Commission's work is discharged usefully and to the satisfaction of charity trustees who for that reason have not put in any evidence to the Committee. It would be a mistake to jettison the present constitution for the sake of finding a way of dealing with a minority of cases. We do think that, particularly in view of the new powers proposed and the existing division of the office between London and Liverpool, there should be an increase in the number of Commissioners from the present three in practice to five, which is already provided for under the Charities Act.

Charities Board

241. We do however consider that an independent Charities Board should be created with a Chairman and members independent of the Charity Commission. Members should come from a wide background which would include service-providing charities, social services, local authorities, business, banking, trusts, health service, education. Members should be brought from different parts of the country, although personal qualities are more important. It is essential that such a board should include members with experience of the new activities in which charities involve themselves, as well as the traditional activities. They would not be appointed directly, except the Chairman, by the Secretary of State but by bodies specified in the legislation.

242. The Charities Board would have the following functions:-

(a) to be consulted by the Charity Commission on matters of general policy.

(b) to advise the Charity Commissioners on matters relating to the policy and administration of the Commission and particularly on:

- (i) the provisional registration of individual charities;
- (ii) the removal of charities from the central register;
- (iii) the conduct of inquiries;
- (iv) the review of charities;
- (v) the conduct of surveys and collection of statistical data.

(c) public relations and the investigation of complaints against the Charity Commissioners.

(d) the appointment of local committees and the conduct of local reviews.

(e) In addition the Charities Board would:

- (i) publish an annual report to the Secretary of State;
- (ii) receive remits from the Secretary of State from time to time and report.

243. The Charity Commission would be charged with providing adequate secretarial staff to the board and would be required to furnish such information as appropriate for the effective performance of these functions.

Regional Responsibilities

244. We think, as appears from the Report already, that there should be employees of standing on the staff of the Charity Commission with regional responsibility who would regularly visit the regions for which they are responsible to preside over the local voluntary committees in connection with parochial and other local charities. There are already staff on the Charity Commission to whom queries from any particular region are referred, but it does not seem that they very frequently visit the areas for which they are responsible or that they have any defined pattern of liaison (see para. 187).

The Inspection of Accounts

245. We think that there should be enough people on the staff of the Charity Commission to step up the review of accounts of charities to the target of once every five years and once every year for new charities in their first three years of provisional registration (see para. 234). There should be at least one qualified accountant on the staff of the Charity Commission to advise on whether accounts are being properly prepared and submitted so as to give all relevant information. Such a member of staff would also be able to advise the Charity Commission on general matters relating to the finance of charities and on specific charities on which enquiries are being conducted.

Staffing of the Charity Commission

246. The staffing of the Charity Commission should enable it to carry out the functions which we have suggested in relation to the renewal of registered charities after three years. Staff should also supervise the survey we have suggested of national charities. We think that consideration should be given to the computerisation of the records of the Charity Commission. We have had evidence suggesting that this would be worth the expense.

Accountability of the Charity Commission

247. The question has been raised as to the accountability of the Charity Commission to Parliament. At present the responsibility of the Home Secretary for the Charity Commissioners is outlined in Schedule I of the Charities Act 1960 in paras. 1 (3), 1 (4), 1 (5). The Act further provides that the Commissioners shall make a report to the Secretary of State annually. However, para. 3 (3) Schedule I states that 'The Commissioners shall have power to regulate their own procedure and, subject to any such regulations and to any directions of the chief commissioner, any one commissioner or any assistant commissioner may act for and in the name of the Commissioners'.

248. A written answer to a Parliamentary Question in the House of Commons on 3rd December 1974 outlined the Secretary of State's responsibilities to Parliament for the Charity Commissioners:-'The (Home Secretary) is answerable to Parliament for the overall administration of the Charity Commissioners as a Public Department, although he has no responsibility for the day-to-day work of the Commissioners. The decisions of the Commissioners, including those relating to the Register of Charities, are subject to review by the courts and not by Ministers'.

249. In effect, the Charity Commissioners are answerable to Parliament in a similar manner to the nationalised industries such as the Post Office and British Rail or bodies such as the British Broadcasting Authority and Civil Aviation Authority. We believe that the Charity Commissioners should not be an exception for three reasons:-

(a) Although exposure to Parliamentary Questions relating to the day-to-day activities of the Charity Commission undoubtedly would sharpen up the administration of any public body, this places an additional administrative burden on the Commission, when the 'envigoration' could be achieved by other means such as the recommendations in paras. 151 and 238 of our report relating to appeals against decisions of the Charity Commission, and to the structure of the Charity Commission.

(b) We believe that the work of charities and the decisions of the Commissioners should be kept out of the political arena regarding their day-to-day operations. The Home Secretary has powers, and is answerable to Parliament for the general efficiency of the Commissioners and for their overall administration and we believe that the Commissioners should, subject to this, be given the same degree of self-regulation as many other public bodies.

(c) It is evident from the Act that the Home Secretary can take the Commissioners to task. Their seeming immunity from intervention may be related rather to successive governments' view of their work than to any lack of powers on the part of the Home Secretary.

These bodies may be the subject of investigation by Parliamentary Select Committees, the Public Accounts Committee and the Expenditure Committee, and as such Parliament has the opportunity to question their operation and policy from time to time.

250. As a result of our recommendations the Home Secretary would have the following additional duties and in the performance of which he would be accountable to Parliament:-

(a) Appointment of the Chairman of the independent Charities Board;

(b) To instruct, from time to time, the Charities Board, to advise him of certain matters relating to the work of the Charity Commission as the Secretary of State shall consider appropriate;

(c) To receive the Annual and Special Reports from the Charities Board.

A More Imaginative Approach

251. The main considerations which we have had in mind in drafting this latter part of the Report are firstly the hope that it will be possible, as a result of the recommendations, to bring a more imaginative and positive attitude to bear on the subject of charities, and secondly, by making a clear distinction between the small local charities and the large national charities, and by decentralising the surveillance of the former to ensure that more time is spent in the years to come on the study of the problems and needs of the larger national charities.

Appendix I

Guidelines in Relation to the Meaning of Charitable Purposes

The following guidelines are intended to be in substitution for the guidelines contained in the preamble to the Statute of Charitable Uses 1601 and the classification of charities contained in the speech of Lord Macnaghten in Pemsel's case. They do not obviate the need for compliance with other criteria of charity such as benefit to a sufficient section of the community and exclusion generally of private profit. The categories of charity contained in the guidelines are not intended to be either exhaustive or immutable but only to be a statement of the types of activity which at the present time should come properly and eminently within the scope of charitable purposes. Any of the said purposes shall be in principle charitable if carried out by UK charities operating abroad.

The expression 'charitable purposes' shall include and shall be deemed always to have included the following purposes, that is to say:-

(a) The relief of poverty howsoever caused and its prevention in suitable cases.

(b) The relief and prevention of sickness and disability, both physical and mental, including:-

- (i) The provision and staffing of hospitals, nursing and convalescent homes and clinics;
- (ii) The promotion of medical research;
- (iii) The provision of advice, treatment or comfort;
- (iv) The establishment of homes, workshops or other centres for the disabled or the mentally or physically handicapped or any other disadvantaged or needy persons.

(c) The relief of the suffering and distress or disability caused by old age, including the provision of homes for the care and maintenance of the old and of housing for old people adapted to their special needs.

(d) The relief of distress caused by natural disasters or sudden catastrophes

(e) The advancement of education, including:

- (i) The provision of schools, colleges, universities, and other like institutions;
- (ii) The establishment of professorships, fellowships, and lectureships;
- (iii) The provision of scholarships, bursaries and prizes;
- (iv) The provision of physical training and sports for young persons both within and without such institutions;
- (v) The education of the public generally (including those not

engaged in full-time study at school, colleges, universities, and other like institutions;

Provided that no attempt is made to influence the public by propaganda

(f) The promotion of research in any field of knowledge seriously deserving to be researched into, whereby the common stock of knowledge can be increased provided that the fruits of such research are intended to be (and are) made available to the public.

(g) The advancement of science (here meaning all recognised branches of learning, and not merely the natural sciences), and the maintenance of institutions therefor, including the support and maintenance of learned societies.

(h) The nurturing of public taste in aesthetic matters, including art, music, literature and fine craftsmanship including facilities for their practice.

(i) The provision and maintenance of museums and art galleries.

(j) The advancement of religion (here meaning belief in and reverence for a divine power) and the practice of the worship of that divinity, including:

- (i) The organisation and carrying out of religious instruction, pastoral and missionary work at home and overseas;
- (ii) The provision and maintenance of buildings for such worship or any other religious use;
- (iii) The payment of stipends to and the provision of houses for ministers of religion, their widows and dependent children: and
- (iv) Other purposes tending to promote the moral or spiritual welfare of the community.

(k) The advancement of ethical and moral teachings and studies.

(l) The provision of social welfare services for those in need of them.

(m) The provision of housing for those in special need.

(n) The protection (including preservation and improvement) of the national heritage whether physical, environmental, artistic, cultural or otherwise.

(o) The promotion of sport and recreation, including the provision of facilities for recreation within the meaning of the Recreational Charities Act 1958.

(p) The welfare of children including prevention of cruelty to them.

(q) The promotion of the social welfare of the family.

(r) The welfare of animals including prevention of cruelty to them.

(s) Rehabilitation and resettlement.

(t) The establishment in life of young people.

(u) The establishment of organisations to assist sections of the community with special needs, for example, one-parent families, single persons with dependants, battered spouses, specially gifted children and immigrants.

(v) Advice giving in suitable circumstances.

(w) The provision of public works for the benefit of the community and the protection of the lives and property of the community (to the extent that these services are inadequately provided for by the State).

(x) The advancement and improvement of the standards of efficiency of industry, commerce and agriculture.

(y) The maintenance and improvement of the efficiency of the fighting forces and the police force and their welfare.

(z) Gifts for the benefit of the inhabitants of a particular place or for the benefit of a particular section of the community.

Appendix II

International Activity (cf paras. 86-88)

(Extract from the Charity Commissioners Report – 1963)

The Commissioners have entertained no doubt that the advancement of religion, the advancement of education and the relief of poverty (the first three heads of charity as classified in the well-known *Pemsel* judgment) are charitable purposes in whatever part of the world they are carried out; but charities must be satisfied in the last case that the poverty to be relieved actually exists in observable cases and is not merely inferred from statistics, and that the measures designed to relieve it, e.g. irrigation, will have a reasonably direct result. (The relief of poverty in this context should be interpreted throughout this letter as including the relief, e.g. of poor refugees or victims of natural disasters). If, however, the measures are directed merely to improving the general economy or standard of living of an overseas community, they probably would be charitable, subject to what is said below about public works within the British Commonwealth.

Other Work for the Benefit of the Community

Charities within the fourth head of the classification in the Pemsel case, i.e. for other purposes beneficial to the community, will be charitable only if of benefit to the community of the United Kingdom. Benefit to the United Kingdom need not be material or direct, but must not be too remote. Charities with general humanitarian objects (e.g. cancer research) can benefit the community of the United Kingdom even if carried on in foreign countries. But where the purposes are the local provision of public works or development projects such as roads and irrigation, these will generally be charitable only if (as I have already said) they are a reasonably direct means to the end of relieving existing poverty in observable cases; but they appear not to be charitable if the purpose is the general economic improvement of another country.

Benefit to the United Kingdom community, however, might arise from charitable purposes for the general benefit of a British Commonwealth country which is in close association with the United Kingdom. But the provision of public works for the general benefit of such a country seemingly could not be charitable if the works were of a class (e.g. a commercial factory) that it would not be charitable to provide in the United Kingdom. It must be repeated that opinions on the law in this field can only be speculative since the decided cases give no clear guidance; but it would appear that the distinction drawn between the Commonwealth countries and foreign sovereign states is based on relationship with the community of the United Kingdom, and it may therefore be charitable to continue to promote the general benefit of countries which are in the process of emerging from dependent to sovereign status. The relief of poverty in foreign states is, of course, charitable if carried out in accordance with para. (1) above.

Co-operation with Overseas Governments
In applying these principles to the question of supplementing the provision made by overseas governments, it would be in accordance with the general scheme of charity partnership with the statutory services in this country for charity trustees to co-operate with the overseas government in pursuing their charitable purpose. But the charity trustees remain responsible for the execution of their trust and the accounting for their expenditure, even, if, as is often the case, they must necessarily engage an overseas agency to act on their behalf. The trustees cannot delegate their responsibilty to others, unless their trust instruments expressly permit them to make outright grants for their charitable purposes to other charitable bodies or to governments. Even where this is done with proper authority, the trustees must take steps to satisfy themselves that the grant will be applied to the particular charitable purpose for which it was originally given.

Accounting by Charity Trustees
Charities which undertake to collect gifts from the public in this country and distribute them among worthwhile charitable projects overseas, owe it to themselves and to the public to arrange a proper system of reporting back on the expenditure of these funds by the receiving organisations. The Commissioners believe that trustees of leading charities of this class are coming to realise that the most satisfactory way of discharging their duty is to obtain reports based on local observation by persons responsible to the trustees, and not merely from the spending authority; and we hope that such a system will become general. Without particularising the form in which accounts should be made up we would remind trustees that, in any event, tax relief on the charity income is conditional on the Inland Revenue being satisfied that it has been applied for charitable purposes only, and they must be prepared to supply the necessary evidence.

It is recognised that these principles may not be easy to apply in practice. In particular, where projects for the indirect benefit of poverty are concerned, trustees should take all reasonable steps to satisfy themselves, on the best evidence available before expending charity funds on a particular project, first, that the poverty demonstrably exists, and second that its relief will not be too remote an effect of the particular project; but even so, there will be borderline cases. In cases of doubt, the Commissioners will be prepared in consultation with the Inland Revenue to do what they can to advise trustees who consult them regarding their duties.

Appendix III

House of Commons Expenditure Committee Comparison of Recommendations

1. After we had commenced our deliberations, the Expenditure Committee of the House of Commons reported on the Charity Commissioners and their accountability. Their recommendations numbering 27 are listed at the end of their report. The matters which the Expenditure Committee considered and the evidence which they heard covered a good deal of the same ground as our own deliberations and it may be useful, therefore, to compare their recommendations with those which we are making in this Report. Accordingly we set out the recommendations of the Expenditure Committee followed by our comments on each recommendation.

Recommendation I
Legislation should be introduced whereby all charities would be required to satisfy the test of 'purposes beneficial to the community'. In the case of those charities formerly admitted under one of the three legal heads, namely, the relief of poverty, the advancement of education and the advancement of religion, they should continue to qualify only if they also satisfy the main criterion.
Comment
We do not think that this recommendation would in any material way alter the law as it exists at the moment. As we understand it, the first three legal heads of charity, namely the relief of poverty, the advancement of education and the advancement of religion, are regarded *ipso facto* as purposes beneficial to the community. A charity, however, under the existing law must benefit a sufficient section of the community so that if the possible beneficiaries are too small a group, that element of public benefit may be lacking. But any provision that the whole community must benefit might eliminate all local charities. The matter is discussed at length in Chapter III of our report.

Recommendation 2
The law should also provide that all political activities in pursuit of a charitable object shall, so long as they remain subordinate to the main purpose of the charity, not endanger its charitable status.
Comment
This recommendation is similar to our recommendation on the same subject, see Chapter IV of our Report.

Recommendation 3
In regard to education, the new test of 'purposes beneficial to the community' should only admit to charitable status those institutions whose educational systems cater for a range of clear educational needs

throughout the whole community. It should also give the courts a more rational and equitable basis on which to interpret the law in respect of grants for the education of children of employees of a firm.

Comment

This is a particular aspect of the point discussed under Recommendation 1. Our own view expressed in para. 47 of our Report is that the decision to abolish private education is a political decision but this political decision should not be obliquely put into force by interfering with charitable status. The question of gifts for the benefit of employees of a firm is discussed in paragraph 37, of our Report.

Recommendation 4

No organisation accepted as a charity before the 1960 Act, the charitable status of which is questionable, should continue to enjoy immunity from investigation by the Charity Commissioners.

Comment

The Charity Commissioners do not at the present time feel any inhibition about reconsidering charitable status if the matter is brought to their attention under the Act. We discuss this in Chapter VI.

Recommendation 5

The public should be made more aware of the important role of the Attorney-General as protector of charitable interests, in the prevention of abuses of charitable status.

Comment

In general we believe that the control should be in the hands of a strengthened Charity Commission and malpractices which involve a breach of criminal law are matters for the police. We approached the Attorney-General but he had no comments to make.

Recommendation 6

In the case of religious institutions, the test of purposes 'beneficial to the community' should be applied in conjunction with any of the first three Macnaghten criteria.

Comment

We believe that any organisation which rejects the idea of a divine purpose but sincerely wishes to study the moral consequences of such rejection is equally of benefit to the community as those organisations who sincerely seek to answer the question whether there is a divine purpose behind the Universe. Sects whose practices include a worship of Satan or which indulge in practices which may be regarded as undesirable may offend against public policy and so forfeit charitable status; a lack of sincerity, if established, would also in our view as the law stands exclude charitable status. We consider the question at length in paras. 51-57 of our Report.

Recommendation 7

The law governing *cy-pres* should be modified so as to enable the Court or the Charity Commissioners when the donor has been dead for a period of time (a) in the case of semi-obsolete charities to amend the objects of the governing instrument in accordance with the public interest and (b) in the case of charities, the return of whose capital assets is too small to be effective, to spend the capital on the purposes of the trust. In such cases, the Commissioners should have reserve powers to override the trustees in the last resort.

Comment

We recommend that it should be made clear that in applying trusts *cy-pres* the Charity Commissioners or the Court have a wide discretion (paras. 189-192) and also that in some cases there should be power to authorise the expenditure of the capital of small trusts (para. 187 (i)). We oppose compulsion in such cases.

Recommendation 8

Local authorities should be empowered under the Local Government Act to compel the amalgamation of charities in appropriate cases, and, if necessary, to wind them up.

Comment

We regard this proposal as quite misconceived. Local charities should be entirely independent of local authorities and it is mainly their fear of municipalisation which hampers their co-operation in the review process under the Charities Act. We discuss at length the pattern of small charities throughout the country and we recommend more enthusiastic persuasion towards amalgamations under the auspices of local voluntary organisations presided over by a representative of the Charity Commissioners but not compulsion (paras. 174-187).

Recommendation 9

A Charities Tribunal should be established to hear appeals from decisions both of the Charity Commissioners and, in special cases, of the Inland Revenue. The cost of the tribunal should be met from a special levy on registration.

Comment

We considered the alternatives of a special tribunal or a system of legal aid for appeals in the High Court in cases where a charity was appealing on a point of law and came down firmly in favour of the latter. However, we felt that an Appeal Tribunal could be a useful adjunct in cases where a charity wished to appeal against administrative decisions of the Charity Commissioners (para. 151). We reject the idea of a levy or registration fee (para. 168).

Recommendation 10

In deserving cases and on important points of law appeals to the High Court against decisions of the Charity Commissioners should be financed from public funds.

Comment

Our system of legal aid would cover proceedings in the High Court and of course, as in all legal aid, there would be power to refuse it in frivolous cases.

Recommendation 11

The principle that all charitable institutions should be eligible for tax privileges, provided the Inland Revenue are satisfied that the funds are properly expended, is endorsed.

Comment

We strongly agree that there should be no discrimination between any charities, particularly on political grounds, in the grant of tax privileges (para. 112).

Recommendation 12

The Layfield Committee should find some satisfactory method of solving the problem whereby local authorities may be unfairly penalised from the system of rating reliefs for charities.

Comment

This problem is considered in paras. 130-132 of our Report and we are gratified to note that the Layfield Committee's suggestion accords with ours.

Recommendation 13

The Charity Commissioners' registration procedure should be expedited by a fresh administrative approach within their existing budgetary provisions. They should produce a variety of model trusts catering for different situations and give them wide circulation. These models should contain draft provisions for the alteration of the trust in the event of its being outdated.

Comment

We would endorse this recommendation generally except that we do feel, in some cases, it should be made a little more difficult for doubtful bodies to be registered. We discuss registration procedures in paras. 139-147. We believe that the Charity Commissioners do have a stock of model deeds for different types of charity and that they are regularly revised.

Recommendation 14

The omission in the law to provide for the registration of certain non-registrable trusts should be remedied.

Comment

This recommendation appears to refer to Section 4(4), (c) of the Charities Act 1960. We discuss this point in paras. 155 and 156 of our Report and make a similar recommendation about this subsection in paragraph 157 of our Report.

Recommendation 15

Serious consideration should be given to bringing all charities, except very small ones, under the jurisdiction of the Charity Commissioners.

Comment

We recommend that all exceptions and exemptions should be reviewed by the Home Secretary (para. 157) and we also recommend that an application to register, except in the case of exempted charities, should be a condition precedent to tax relief (para. 153). There do however appear to be sound reasons for some of the exemptions.

Recommendation 16
More women should be encouraged to participate as trustees of charities.
Comment
We do not specifically consider this point but would not in any way dissent from it.

Recommendation 17
The procedures governing transfers of property between charities (or between charities and local authorities) should be applied less rigorously and with greater discretion than between charitable and non-charitable bodies.
Comment
We do not mention this point in our Report. Our belief is that the Charity Commissioners do take a reasonable view in the case of transfers between charities.

Recommendation 18
The Charity Commissioners should send to all trustees a circular setting out in simple terms all the considerations which they regard as relevant in the disposal of property.

Recommendation 19
Each trustee of a newly registered charity should be sent a brochure outlining his responsibilities.
Comment on These Two Recommendations
We agree that the Charity Commissioners should give the maximum possible help and advice to trustees; but without incurring unnecessary expenses.

Recommendation 20
A small annual registration fee should be introduced, possibly on a sliding scale. Failure to register, to submit accounts regularly to the Commissioners and to pay the annual fee should result in loss of taxation and other fiscal benefits.
Comment
We do not agree in principle to a registration fee (paragraph 168). We make proposals for a more effective accounting system in paragraphs 225-234.

Recommendation 21
Charities on first registration should be placed on probation for a trial period of five years.
Comment
We do not think that all new charities should automatically be given a provisional registration, but we do think that the Charity Commissioners should have a discretion to make registration provisional and in these cases we think there should be a review after three years (paragraphs 140-147).

Recommendation 22
A standardised form of account should be evolved and a computerised system introduced to facilitate and expedite the submission of annual accounts by trustees and their scrutiny by the Charity Commissioners, the cost of the latter to be met from the special levy on registration.
Comment
In view of the vast differences between one charity and another, a standardised form of account may not be appropriate in all cases. We discussed this problem and computerisation in paras. 231, 232, and 246. We do not agree with a levy on registration (para. 168).

Recommendation 23
The Chief Charity Commissioner should be selected from a wide field of choice, including the Civil Service, the professions, private industry and the voluntary and social services.
Comment
We are of the view that the present constitution of the Charity Commission works well and should not be jettisoned for the sake of finding a way of dealing with a minority of cases (para. 240). We do, however, propose that an independent Charities Board be created to advise the Charity Commissioners, membership of which should be drawn from a wide field of choice.

Recommendation 24
A standing selection panel should be set up to advise the Home Secretary on the appointments of all Charity Commissioners. The panel should be drawn from both the voluntary organisations and local authority social service departments.
Comment
We do not agree with this recommendation. The ordinary appointments procedures should be adopted in preference to the creation of a new body (para. 240).

Recommendation 25
A special task force, drawn from the social services and voluntary organisations, under a fourth Charity Commissioner should be established for the purpose of carrying out local reviews and to undertake investigations into a charity when need arises.
Comment
We make a recommendation for local committees drawn from voluntary organisations chaired by a representative of the Charity Commissioners to carry out local reviews and undertake local supervision in paragraph 185. We would prefer a number of local committees to a single roving task force.

Recommendation 26
The Home Secretary should answer Parliamentary Questions on Charities and the Charity Commissioners. The resurrection of the post of Parliamentary Commissioner as a substitute for the Home Secretary in this capacity would not be acceptable.

Comment

We think that as regards Parliamentary Questions the Charity Commission should be in the same position as nationalised bodies. We suggest certain new functions for the Home Secretary in relation to which he would be answerable to Parliament (para. 250).

Recommendation 27

The Home Secretary should have wider powers to make Orders and Statutory Instruments in respect of the Charity Commissioners and Charities, subject to affirmative Resolutions of the House.

Comment

If this means that the Home Secretary can amend charity law by Statutory Instrument, then we would dissent strongly from any such proposition. The scope of charities should not be the subject of political decisions.

Appendix IV

Individuals and Organisations from which the Committee received Written Evidence

Accountancy Age
Advertising Standards Authority
Air League, The
Sir Max Aitken
Allardyce
Alternative Society
Amnesty International (British Section)
Andersen, Arthur & Co.
Anglesey Rural Community Council
Architects Benevolent Society
Arts Council
Associated Society of Locomotive Engineers and Firemen
Association of Charity Officers
Association of Corporate Trustees
Association of District Councils
Association of Scientific, Technical and Managerial Staffs (NCSS Group)
Association of Social Research Organisations
Baptist Peace Fellowship
Baring Bros. & Co. Ltd.
Barnardo's Homes
Barristers Benevolent Association
Bartlett, Walters & Parry (on behalf of Charnwood Community Council)
Lord Beaumont of Whitley
Beit Trust
Bingham, J.B.
Birkenhead Council for Voluntary Service
Birmingham Charities Review (Mr Douglas King, Director)
Blaney Baker, K.M.
Board of Inland Revenue
Bradley, K.
Bristol Council for Voluntary Service
British Association for the Hard of Hearing
The British Campaign for Peace in Vietnam
The British Council
British Epilepsy Association
British Federation of Music Festivals
British Heart Foundation Appeal
British Hospitals Contributory Schemes Associations
British Polio Fellowship
British Red Cross
Lord Brockway
Brown, Mrs E.M.A.

Bush, C.S.
Bywater, B.
Cadbury Trust
Carnegie UK Trust
Central and East Fife Co-operative Society Limited
Central Council of Physical Recreation
Centre-file (Northern) Ltd.
Chapman, Dr. Richard A.
Charities Aid Foundation
Charity Commissioners
Charity Law Reform Committee
Charlton, Nial
Chartered Institute of Public Finance and Accountancy
Cheam Invicta Club
Child Poverty Action Group
Children's Society
Christian Aid
Churches Council of Health and Healing
Churches Main Committee
Church of England
Civic Trust
Civil and Public Services Association
Cockayne, W.N.
Commercial Travellers Benevolent Institution
Commonwealth Society for the Deaf
Community Council for Lincoln
Community Council for Suffolk
Rt. Hon. Lord Crayton, CBE
Cripplegate Foundation
Customs and Excise
Darby, D.
Department of Education and Science
Department of the Environment
Department of Health and Social Security
Department of Prices and Consumer Protection
Department of Trade
Devon and Cornwall Constabulary Widows and Orphans and Compassionate Fund
Disabled Living Foundation
Donald, Wm.
Dudley Council for Voluntary Service
Durham County Council
Elderly Invalids Fund
Equity – Chas. Farrell, Treasurer
Family Welfare Association
Farming Scholarship Trust, UK
Farrell, C.
Fawcett, F.G.
Febeson and Arkeid
Fellowship of Reconciliation

Friend
Foreign and Commonwealth Office
Gampell, Michael
Gerard, David
Gingerbread
Gloucester Review Organiser – L.R. Duirs
Glover, G.N.
Glyndebourne Festival Opera
Goheen, Robert F., Chairman of Council of Foundation Inc (USA)
Goodhard, Dr C.B.
Hamel, G.P., Cheltenham Co-Operative Charities
Hammersmith Council of Social Service
Hastings Community Service Council
Hawkins, Leslie J.
Help The Aged
Hesslewood, F.E.
Hildrew, Peter
Hodge Charitable Trust, The Jane and Julian
Home Office, Voluntary Services Unit
Hondius, Dr F.
Hooker, Michael & Associates Ltd.
Horder Centres for Arthritics
Housing Corporation, The
Humanist Association, British
Humber Keel Trust
Imperial Cancer Research Fund
Independent Labour Party – Wolverhampton and Bristol Branch
Independent Schools Advisory Service
Independent Schools Joint Committee
Inland Waterways Association
International Friendship League
Institute of Chartered Secretaries and Administrators
Institute of Road Transport Engineers
Johnston, Joseph A.
Justice – British Section of the International Commission of Jurists
Sir Emmanuel Kaye, CBE
'Lancashire Evening Post'
Law Society, The
'Lest We Forget' Association
Letchworth and District Council of Social Service
Leukaemia Research Fund
Lewis Dwellings Trust, The Samuel
Lincolnshire Community Council
Lingfield Hospital School
Livingston Booth, J.D.
London Boroughs Association
London Borough of Merton
London Council of Social Service
London Symphony Orchestra
Lovecy, Dr A.L.

Lower Sapey House Association
Macphair, Ian S.
Make The Children Happy
Manchester Council for Voluntary Service
Manchester and Salford Council of Social Service
Maurice, E.E.
Methodist Church Division of Social Responsibility
Ministry of Overseas Development
Multiple Sclerosis Society
Munday, Diane
Museums Association, The
National Adult School Union
National Association of Almhouses
National Association of Boys Clubs
National Association of Leagues of Hospital Friends
National Association of Local Councils
National Association for Mental Health
National Corporation for the Care of Old People
National Council for Civil Liberties
National Council of Women
National Farmers Union
National Federation of Young Farmers Clubs
National Federation of Housing Associations
National Gipsy Education Council
National Playing Fields Association
National Peace Council
National Secular Society
National Society for Clean Air
National Society for the Prevention of Cruelty to Children
National Youth Bureau
Newspaper Press Fund
Nightingale, Benedict
Nokes, J.H.
Northcote Children's Emigration Fund
Northamptonshire Review of Charities
Nuclear Disarmament Campaign
Nuffield Foundation
Nuffield Nursing Homes Trust
Old Age Pensioners Club
Old Cleeve Memorial Cottage
Ministry of Overseas Development
Oxfam
Oxford Rural Community Council, Review Organiser
Oxfordshire County Council
Pearce, Penelope and Alec Samuels
Pendlebury's Charity for Orphans, Sir Ralph
Performing Animals Defence League
Phillips & Buck
Phillips, E. Hereward
Phillpott, Mike

Pilborough, G.A.
Pollard, Thos & Co.
Pre-Retirement Association
Pre-School Playgroups Association
Psoriasis Association
Queen Elizabeth's Foundation for the Disabled
Queen Elizabeth's Hospital for Children
RSPCA
Rampton, A.
Rationalist Press Association Ltd.
Responsible Society, The
Returned Volunteer Action
Ripon Council for Voluntary Service
Robson, Eric
Rogers, Miss Angela
Ross, Leonard & Co.
Rothschild, Edmund
Rowntree Memorial Trust, Joseph
Rowntree Social Service Trust, Joseph
Royal British Legion
Royal National Institute for the Blind
Royal National Lifeboat Institution
Royal National Lifeboat Institution – Nottingham and District Branch
Royal Medical Foundation of Epsom College
Royal Society of Medicine
Royal Wolverhampton School
Bertrand Russell Peace Foundation Ltd.
St John's Ambulance Association and Brigade
Salter, Ann
Salvation Army, The
Save The Children Fund
Sefton Council for Voluntary Service
Seven Springs Cheshire Home
Rev. Michael Scott – Africa Bureau
Scottish Society for the Prevention of Vivisection
Shelter
Silverstein, Leonard, Exec. Director – Committee of Private Philanthropy and Public Need, U.S.A.
Sinclair, M.M.
Slough Council for Voluntary Service
Social Service Advertising Ltd.
Soldiers' Sailors' and Airmen's Families Association
Spastics Society
Sports Council
Standing Conference of British Organisations for Aid to Refugees
Stockport Council for Voluntary Service
Sunter, Ian Anderson
Surrey County Cricket Club
Target Consultants Ltd.
The Theosophical Society in England

Toc H
Treasury Solicitor
United Kingdom Immigrants Advisory Service
United Kingdom Farming Scholarship Trust
United Nations Association
United Reformed Church
Variety Club of Great Britain
Voluntary Animal Welfare Society
Voluntary and Christian Service
Walker, P.P.
War On Want
Waveney District Council
Wells, P. Arthur & Associates
Wells, T.C.E.
West Somerset District Council
West Yorkshire Youth Association
Whinney, Capt. R.F.
Williams, Isla
Wimbledon Guild of Social Welfare
Wings of Friendship
Worcestershire Rural Community Council
Workers Educational Trust
Writers and Scholars Education Trust
YWCA
York University, Institute of Social and Economic Research (Messrs. Culyer, Wiseman and Posnett)
Youth Hostels Association, England and Wales
Several Anonymous Submissions were received

Appendix V

Individuals and Organisations from which the Committee took Oral Evidence

Alternative Society
Amnesty International (British Section)
Association of District Councils
Association of Metropolitan Authorities
British Epilepsy Association
British Humanist Association
Cancer Research Campaign
Canine Defence League
Charity Law Reform Committee
Charity Commissioners
Institute of Chartered Accountants in England and Wales
Gingerbread
Gloucestershire Review Organiser
Mr. Brian Gould, MP
Dr. F. Hondius
Hooker (Michael) & Associates Ltd
Inland Revenue
Mr. T. Kingdom
Mr. J.D. Livingston Booth
National Council for Civil Liberties
National Playing Fields Association
Nightingale, Benedict
Oxfordshire County Council
Oxfordshire Charity Review Organiser
Sports Council, The
United Nations Association

A Minority Report by Ben Whitaker

1. Initial Premise

I feel more strongly than some of my colleagues that our approach and recommendations should be determined by present needs rather than by the past history of charities. The views of 1601 and of Lord Macnaghten in 1891 are of historical interest, but to my mind the real question for us should be to define the role of charities in the last quarter of the twentieth century. The legal concept of charity must develop in pace with the ever-changing requirements of society and not be governed – as Sir Arthur Hobhouse, the prescient nineteenth century Charity Commissioner warned against – by dead hands from the grave. 'Why should a man, whose opinion no one regarded in life, be able to dictate how posterity shall use part of the wealth they make centuries after he is dead?' he asked. Many problems of today, let alone the ascertainable future, cannot be properly tackled by charities if they are to be crabbed and confined by the case law of the past (race relations, for example, were not an issue in 1891): present-day criteria and priorities ought to be decided, especially in times of increasing change, by contemporary society and not by judges governed by precedents embalming the value judgements of our forbears.

2. The Public Subsidy for Charities

It is crucial at the outset to distinguish between, on the one hand, the right of an individual to give his or her money or services in any way he or she chooses (which no one would restrict), and on the other hand the distinctly different principle of society being compelled to subsidise this conduct with tax relief and the other benefits and privileges accorded to legal charities. This subsidy is no minor item: the House of Commons Expenditure Committee last year estimated that the tax exemptions alone of charities costs well over £100 million per annum, and that their assets amount to a minimum of £2,500-£3,000 million; while another source estimates that in 1975 charities received £410 million. Public funds unfortunately are neither limitless nor self-raising: and fiscal benefits, which enrich private charities above the natural level provided by their donors, must inevitably be at the expense of democratically determined public programmes – many of which today are badly in need of finance.

3. The Criterion for Charitable Status

The ideal criterion for charitable status would be any purpose beneficial to the community – provided always any such benefit was equally accessible to all members of the community who wish to avail themselves of it. But since charitable resources and the public's ability to give tax relief are both limited, I believe the first priority should be to concentrate these primarily **on deprivation and the disadvantaged**.

These should here be interpreted to include the results of not only poverty and sickness (physical and mental), but also of lack of human rights and education. While the duty of mutual care in human society is shared by and extends to the whole community, I consider it right that if the public is to be compulsorily taxed, it should be able to determine the priorities to which the limited supplies of public funds are devoted. Private benefactors who prefer to help those people who are not disadvantaged should be of course, free to do so, but they ought not to assume that the remainder of society should be compulsorily made to assist them: anyone is entitled to start a fund to benefit, for instance, distressed gentlefolk or officers' mess silver (to cite two current types of charities which in my opinion should cease to be so), but they should not conscript taxpayers to contribute involuntary subsidies. Otherwise, charity could result in the redistribution of resources from the poorer taxpayer to those who are already more privileged – a policy of which I fail to see the logic, let alone the justice.

A Tribunal to Interpret Definition: If the legal tail is not to wag the charitable dog again in the future, it is essential that the ongoing interpretation of any new definition should be in the hands of a Tribunal, a majority of whose members are laymen and women (in the sense of not being lawyers) with an uncloistered knowledge of the altering problems of contemporary society.

4. The Need for Charities in Society

Certain responsibilities are too important to continue to be met, as they traditionally have been, by private charities and can only really be undertaken by the state. The adequacy of a national lifeboat service, for example, should not have to depend on the caprice of donors, any more than the prevention of cruelty to children should have to rely on the collecting boxes of the NSPCC. Promoting the efficiency of the armed forces should not be a charitable purpose, but the responsibility of the Ministry of Defence. But I agree with my colleagues that some charitable trusts can play a very important role in a free society, not only as pioneers of policies and experimental catalysts, but also as independent critics of established thinking and programmes. It is one of the healthiest attributes of a social democracy that the state should, in fact, subsidise such alternatives, provided this does not compromise their independence.* Charities possess the capacity, in microcosm, to suggest re-shapings of society. Less often they possess the energy or inclination to use their resources and independence in any such way. Too many vie to be part of the establishment. But agencies supported wholly by government finance are likely to be even more reluctant to support fundamental self-criticism or unpopular and unfashionable causes.

5. Overseas Charities

I firmly agree that charity should not stop at national boundaries: the

*Perhaps I should declare a personal interest in that I work as director, chairman and trustee of different charities.

concept that mankind's needs are indivisible is reinforced by the example of recent ecological crises.

6. A Suggested Definition of Charity

In tackling most problems, preventive action is preferable to palliatives as well as generally being easier than attempts at a cure (see Political Activities, paragraph 21 below), and therefore prevention as well as relief should be encouraged. I would recommend that the essential ingredient of the modern definition of charity – which should be as simple and clear as possible, yet sufficiently broad and flexible to take account of the changing needs of society – should focus primarily on **the prevention and relief of deprivation (whether physical, mental or social), provided always any resultant benefit is equally accessible to all relevant members of the community who wish to avail themselves of it (irrespective of race, sex, religion, politics or social class).**

7. Exclusive Charities

In explanation of this last proviso, I would regard it as contrary to public policy to subsidise bodies or organisations which discriminate on grounds of race, religion, gentility, politics or sex (for example, I consider the practice of public schools which operate a Jewish quota to be distasteful). But I must also dissent strongly from my colleagues' views about **costly fees, subscriptions or charges for services** (Majority Report, paras. 46-49). The effect of some of these at present is to restrict the benefit of some so-called charities (not only schools and hospitals) to those people who are generally already most privileged financially and socially. The fact that this is achieved often at the expense of poorer taxpayers means that the net result can be a redistribution of advantages from the less well off to the rich – a concept of charity which did not occur even to Jonathan Swift, and requires his pen to do justice to. With all due respect to my colleagues on this Committee, I cannot help feeling it is unfortunate that – as on so many committees in this country which consider public policies – there is not a single representative of the working-class majority of society among our members. I am wholly persuaded by the evidence we received arguing that in regard to hospitals charitable status should be allowed **to only those institutions whose work is intended by its objects directly and primarily (but not exclusively) to be of benefit to the poor, and which does not charge fees to any or all of those persons intended to benefit from the work of the institution at such a level that the effect in practice is to exclude those with average or below average incomes;** and that this same principle is as valid in respect of schools, universities, artistic performances and other charitable institutions as it is of hospitals and clinics – some of which at present are open to the public only in the sense that the Savoy Hotel is accessible to all.

8. Education

While the future of private education itself is a separate issue to be decided elsewhere, the distribution of the benefits of charitable status in the educational field does fall within the principles to be considered by this Committee. Here I dissent from my colleagues' view in paragraph 60 and 61 of the Majority Report, that **financially exclusive schools** be allowed to continue to enjoy charitable status, and agree instead with the unanimous recommendation of the all-party House of Commons Expenditure Committee (in paragraph 50 of their 1975 Report) that charitable status should be given only to those institutions **'which manifestly devote the education they provide towards meeting a clear range of educational needs throughout the whole community'.** Whilst there are clear arguments for subsidising experiments, variety, and the supply of special needs in education when their benefits are open to all children and students I fail to see why the community should be compelled to support financially exclusive schools which are restricted largely to those families who are already most privileged.

9. Religion

Although in the past charity often had religious origins, today religion and charity are two distinct concepts which may or may not necessarily coincide. There are clear practical arguments in favour of concluding that religious bodies should be granted charitable status only in so far as they carry out otherwise charitable activities: e.g. for their work in relieving poverty, but not for providing vestments. Deciding which religious practices are too anti-social to be allowed charitable benefits is an invidious task.

10. Religious Propaganda

If charitable status, is however, to be granted also to religious bodies advocating beliefs and propaganda, it obviously must in fairness, equally be available to similar non-religious bodies. The present position cannot be defended whereby churches and the Lord's Day Observance Society conduct propaganda and political campaigns with the help of the tax benefits of charitable status, while, for example, the Humanist Trust or the National Secular Society is forbidden to do so. If the propagation of a religious philosophy is deemed charitable in equity so must also the advocacy of humanistic liberalism, Marxism, or other ethical and political philosophies. Otherwise, the satisfactory test of a religion in this context poses superhuman problems: what law court or human agency empowered to demarcate charitable status is competent to judge the validity of a religion or the genuineness of a new guru* or claimant to be a new Messiah? What would have been the verdict of an early Charity Commission on Jesus Christ, or the first Christians, or the Inquisition? Surely these are questions for a God, rather than for any earthly agency or Mammon; and therefore, whereas the comparative study of different religions, ethics and philosophies is a part of education, religious proselytising cannot be termed charitable except in so far as other propaganda is allowed to be so. It is relevant to note that the Religious Education Council has recently proposed that Non-Supernatural Philosophies should in future be included in the syllabus of schools' religious education.

*If applicants must produce a satisfactory miracle, then Mr Uri Geller might appear a strong claimant.

11. Accountability
Charitable status is a privilege granted by the public, not a private right. All charities which enjoy any tax or legal advantage should, without exception or exemption, be obliged (a) to be registered and submit themselves to the Charity Commission's supervision; and (b) annually to file audited accounts and a report of its policy and activities, which should be freely available for public inspection. Any charity failing to do so should forfeit its tax relief, and after a specified period should cease to be a charity.

12. Research
A copy of any research report or findings, financed from charitable funds, should also be available for public reading.

13. Trustees
There is a strong case for the appointment of a trustee to be limited to a period of, say, six years in any one term, in order to facilitate the introduction of fresh ideas and energy into a charity. Not enough women, or working class, or younger people or members of minorities are trustees.

14. A further proviso could be to require a charity to re-register every, say, 20 years, in order that its continuing relevance could be demonstrated.

15. In guarding against the fraudulent or the supine, prevention is preferable to shutting the stable door too late: one solution would be to have on each charity one public trustee who was appointed to safeguard the interests of society. (The City Parochial Foundation, for example, has five Crown trustees, who act not as delegates but exercise their own independent judgements.) This would help prevent incompetence, irrelevance or inertia which at present sometimes come to light – if at all – years too late; though it would be essential to have public trustees only as a small minority on the board of any one charity. Society has an obvious interest in charities, financed partly with public money, being properly run and accountable; equally it is crucial to safeguard their independence from government control.

16. Charity Commission: Lay Element
It would be beneficial if not only, as the Nathan Committee recommended (Cmd. 8710) 16 years ago, there should be an expert lay Advisory Committee (whose advice should be binding on the Charity Commission regarding registration), but that the Commission itself should also have an infusion of a substantial lay element (i.e. people who are neither lawyers nor civil servants). We received evidence that the Commission at present seems 'legalistic', 'slow', 'remote', and 'oppressive in some matters, weak in others'. 'It is difficult over registration, especially of new-type social welfare organisations, and insists on ridiculous old-fashioned wording in the constitution, redolent of the eighteenth century, mystifying and repugnant to the

layman'. Other witnesses told us that the Commission could do much more to advise charities in ordinary lay English of the new legislation affecting charities, of financial and other services available to charities to help them to be more effective, and to tell trustees more fully of their duties.

17. Rationalisation

In particular I believe also much more effective action is overdue, and should now be taken, to rationalise the plethora of tiny obsolescent charities. Witnesses told us **'the policy of the 1960 Act to encourage the little and the obsolete charities to modernise and to combine has failed and compulsory measures are now called for. In these hard times, no charity funds can be left idle'.** As the 'New Law Journal' commented in July 1971, 'the Commission's power to impose schemes on trustees who refused to bring their objects into line with social needs has never been achieved, no penalties exist for failure to register – many charities have failed to do so . . . The commissioners themselves have publicly acknowledged their inability to scrutinise the accounts of registered charities on a regular basis consistent with their responsibilities'.

The fact that, 16 years after the Act, over half the charities registered with the Charity Commission have an annual income of less than £50 and nearly 25 per cent have an income of less than £5, speaks for itself.

18. Finance

I believe it is incumbent upon us as a Committee which is proposing improvements in the supervision of charities also to propose how such reforms should be financed. On too many occasions public suggestions are made for new measures requiring increases in civil servants and administrative machinery at the same time as – often the same voices – demand restrictions on public expenditure. Therefore, unlike my colleagues, I believe it is right that the better supervision of, and help for, charities which we recommend should be financed by a modest levy on charities, and I believe this is most justly shared on the basis of a small proportion of each charity's finances.

19. Corporate Charity

I disagree with the proposal, in para. 124 of the Majority Report, that there should be any upper limit to charitable contributions from companies. If such donations are right in principle, as I agree that they are, companies should be allowed – and indeed encouraged – to give (as a very few of them do now) any amount up to 100 per cent of their profits.

20. I also think that the views of employees as well as directors and shareholders should play a part in making such decisions (as happens, for example, at the Scott Bader Commonwealth Company at Wellinborough, Northants).

21. Political Activities by Charities

I believe it is not only the right but in fact the duty of charities in many areas to act as political pressure groups, and that legislation must end the present uncertainty about this forthwith. The days of confining charities to pouring soup into faulty old bottles should be consigned to the past; such cosmetic philanthropy can in fact be capable of postponing the more fundamental reforms that may be needed. Campaigning for changes in laws is often not only the most cost-effective but virtually the only policy for organisations like the Disablement Income Group or the Finer Action Committee to adopt: they cannot hope to finance the needs of disabled people or of one-parent families themselves. To further illustrate this point, it is worth recalling that when the British government cut its overseas aid programme by £20m in 1966 it did so by a sum greater than the total of all Oxfam's spending since its inception in 1942. It could be argued that if, instead of financing projects abroad, Oxfam concentrated on education, propaganda and political pressure in Britain which resulted in the government increasing its present net aid budget by even 10 per cent, vastly more 'poverty, distress and suffering' would be relieved overseas.

22. Politics – as distinct from party politics – being a charity's responsibilty, one important role for contemporary charities can be, for instance, to act as lobbies for the deprived, the unorganised, or the unpopular. They can exert pressure on behalf of the inarticulate and those most in need: to campaign, for example, to make state schools as good as some (at present) charitable private schools are, or public libraries as good as the (at present charitable) London Library. While declaring my own interest in a number of organisations concerned with human rights, I know that support for such causes is shared by people of all party politics and of none: concern for justice, freedom of expression, mercy, etc., is felt by members of widely differing political views. I therefore cannot share the dilemma expressed in paragraph 102 of the Majority Report. It would be ironic if (as at present) the prevention of cruelty to animals continued to be encouraged with charitable status for the RSPCA, while the prevention of cruelty to humans is not because similar status is withheld from Amnesty. I was impressed by the evidence of the then Permanent Secretary at the Department of the Environment, Sir James Jones: 'In the formulation of Departmental policy we are very considerably influenced, both at ministerial and at official level, by the views of charitable organisations . . . I would not wish to claim that we always see eye to eye with these bodies, since they properly see it as part of their function to identify departmental shortcomings. But I think we would always be prepared to admit that our policy-thinking would be narrower and poorer in quality without the stimulus arising from our contact with pressure groups of this kind. We would not therefore favour any argument that charities should abjure lobbying and should be made to stick to their more limited role of direct action in providing housing or relieving distress'.

23. The current opaque position, in any event, does allow some political activity – but only on an anomalous and unfairly selective basis. On many occasions tax-exempt Churches campaign and try to influence both the government and voters about laws concerning – for example – divorce, abortion, birth control and other questions which affect even those who are not their co-religionists. Futhermore the present restrictions, real or assumed, result in most charities having to support the status quo, which in itself is a political attitude. The campaigning of the Lord's Day Observance Society (a charity) which persistently lobbies Parliament, is one active example: others play a similar role passively. Of course charities existing to defend current policies must be treated equally with those seeking change.

24. I am not attracted by the suggestion (in paragraph 105) of continuing artificially to divide an organisation's political from its charitable activities. It should not be public policy to put a premium on hypocrisy.

25. The recently introduced government finance for the major political parties breaks a traditional embargo on state help, but this is of course limited only to the established ones with Parliamentary seats. (It would have excluded the Labour Party 80 years ago, or the Scottish or Welsh Nationalist Parties 20 years ago.) There is, therefore, an additional case in fairness for also finding a way to give some financial help to non-established or new smaller groups, including those not interested in parliamentary representation.